CONTENTS

World map

EUROPE & THE MIDDLE EAST
A group of Gypsies in England.
Europe, together with the Middle
East, covers an area of 19.6 million
sq km. It has a population of
almost 1,100 million people.

AFRICA
A Pygmy from Zaire.
Africa is the second-largest
continent, after Asia. It
covers an area of over 30
million sq km and has a
population of more than
750 million people.

ASIA
Ainu people on Hokkaido. Asia,
the world's largest continent, has
an area of 44 million sq km. Its
population of almost 3,500 million
is also the largest of any continent.

THE FROZEN NORTH
A Saami woman in Finland. The part of the Frozen North lying inside the Arctic Circle covers an area of 36 million sq km. About one million indigenous people live there.

NORTH AMERICA
A group of Native American children in the USA. North America, including Mexico and the countries of Central America, covers an area of 24 million sq km.

SOUTH AMERICA
A Yanomami girl. South America has a population of 330 million spread over an area of 17.9 million sq km.

AUSTRALIA & NEW ZEALAND
A Maori warrior from New Zealand. Australia and New Zealand have a combined population of just over 22 million people, and an area of 7.9 million sq km.

5

How to Use this Atlas

BIG REGION PAGE

On the pages showing large region maps you will find a globe. This shows you where in the world the continent is situated.

The text on these pages introduces you to the general situation in the region, and tells you some of the common problems that threatened cultures there have.

The *Wayland Atlas of Threatened Cultures* contains information about almost 1,000 different peoples around the world. You can find out in detail about nearly thirty of these: people from various kinds of environment who live many different kinds of life.

There are two kinds of map and two sorts of text in this book.

The text on the people pages tells you about particular groups: their way of life and how it is threatened with destruction. If you want to know where there are other groups suffering from similar threats, you can find out using the key to the map of the continent. If you want to find out about the threats to other groups living in the same area, you can also use the continent map to do that.

On many of the people pages there are lists of other groups who have similar problems to the ones you have just read about. You can find where these other groups live by looking at the continent map at the start of the chapter.

THE FROZEN NORTH

All indigenous peoples in the Arctic live in countries where there is a non-indigenous majority. These populations live to the south and their governments regard the Arctic as a source of oil, gas, metals and other natural resources.

But for the many small groups of indigenous peoples who have adapted themselves over thousands of years to its extreme harshness, the Arctic is their homeland. Here, where crops cannot be grown, humans have been able to survive only by hunting large animals. The Saami and the peoples of Siberia have hunted reindeer and elk, and in recent centuries they have domesticated reindeer into large herds. In Greenland and across northern North America, the Inuit (Eskimo) peoples live along the coast, where they hunt seals, whales and walrus.

Because their food is spread out over a wide area, Arctic animals migrate huge distances. So even a tiny human population needs thousands of square kilometres to hunt and herd. The extraction of minerals and other natural resources by southern industries cuts across the animals' migration routes and pollutes the environment.

This century, throughout the Arctic, indigenous cultures have been undermined by government schemes that have concentrated the scattered hunters into large villages and sent their children to grim boarding schools in distant towns. The children have lost contact with their parents and with their own culture, and become incapable of hunting or living on the land. The results have been widespread despair, alcoholism and suicide. But since the 1970s, Arctic peoples have started to demand compensation for resources taken from them and for environmental damage. They have also campaigned for measures to preserve their languages and cultures.

Though they live far from big cities, Arctic peoples are seriously threatened by pollution carried in the air from the industrialized south. In Canada, Inuit women's breast milk contains high levels of mercury, while in Russia and Scandinavia huge areas have been contaminated by radioactive fallout from nuclear explosions. But a major threat to Arctic cultures comes from some environmentalists and animal rights supporters in Europe and America. They campaign against seal hunting or whaling, without understanding the unique relationship between Arctic peoples and the animals with which they live and on which they depend to keep their cultures alive.

GIVE ME BACK MY LAND

'The loggers even cut down all the trees on the tribal cemetery, thus ruining the final resting place. In all his 76 years, my father had not once plucked a fir needle or a leaf, not a blade of grass unnecessarily on his land, on the land of his ancestors.

'"What do you want, old man?" I ask my father. "Can I help you?"

'"I don't want anything," he says after a long silence. "Only my land. Give me back my land where I can graze my reindeer, hunt game and catch fish. Give me my land where my deer are not attacked by stray dogs and poachers, where the rivers and lakes have no oil slicks – just a patch of my own land."

'What can I say in reply?'

Yeremei Aipin, a Khant writer from Siberia

10

PEOPLE PAGE

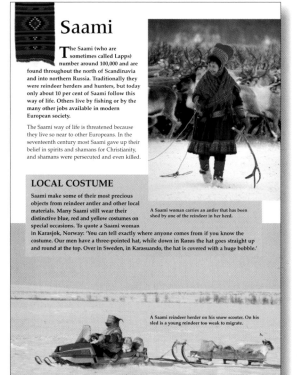

Saami

The Saami (who are sometimes called Lapps) number around 100,000 and are found throughout the north of Scandinavia and into northern Russia. Traditionally they were reindeer herders and hunters, but today only about 10 per cent of Saami follow this way of life. Others live by fishing or by the many other jobs available in modern European society.

The Saami way of life is threatened because they live so near to other Europeans. In the seventeenth century most Saami gave up their belief in spirits and shamans for Christianity, and shamans were persecuted and even killed.

LOCAL COSTUME

Saami make some of their most precious objects from reindeer antler and other local materials. Many Saami still wear their distinctive blue, red and yellow costumes on special occasions. To quote a Saami woman in Karasjok, Norway: 'You can tell exactly where anyone comes from if you know the costume. Our men have a three-pointed hat, while down in Røros the hat goes straight up and round at the top. Over in Sweden, in Karasuando, the hat is covered with a huge bobble.'

A Saami woman carries an antler that has been shed by one of the reindeer in her herd.

A Saami reindeer herder on his snow scooter. On his sled is a young reindeer too weak to migrate.

BIG REGION PAGE

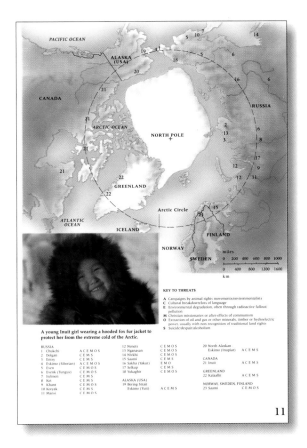

A young Inuit girl wearing a hooded fox fur jacket to protect her from the extreme cold of the Arctic.

These big maps show different groups from a particular region. Where the groups live is shown on the map by a number: next to the map is a key that tells you the names of the groups shown by the number. The key also uses letters to show some of the main threats to the way of life of each group. You can find the location of a group that you have heard about by using the key, then the map. Or you can find groups suffering under similar threats by looking at the key, then finding out their name and location.

PEOPLE PAGE

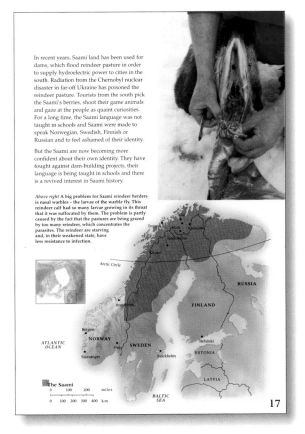

In recent years, Saami land has been used for dams, which flood reindeer pasture in order to supply hydroelectric power to cities in the south. Radiation from the Chernobyl nuclear disaster in far-off Ukraine has poisoned the reindeer pasture. Tourists from the south pick the Saami's berries, shoot their game animals and gaze at the people as quaint curiosities. For a long time, the Saami language was not taught in schools and Saami were made to speak Norwegian, Swedish, Finnish or Russian and to feel ashamed of their identity.

But the Saami are now becoming more confident about their own identity. They have fought against dam-building projects, their language is being taught in schools and there is a revived interest in Saami history.

Above right A big problem for Saami reindeer herders is nasal warbles – the larvae of the warble fly. This reindeer calf had so many larvae growing in its throat that it was suffocated by them. The problem is partly caused by the fact that the pastures are being grazed by too many reindeer, which concentrates the parasites. The reindeer are starving and, in their weakened state, have less resistance to infection.

The maps on these pages show you where a particular people lives, the main towns, rivers and roads, and the hills and valleys. In the corner of these maps you will find a small map of the continent, which shows you where the area of the bigger map is located.

Mexico and Guatemala have so many peoples packed into such a small area that each of these countries has its own map, showing all the peoples who live there.

Threatened Cultures Around the World

All over the world, from the icy wastelands of the Arctic Circle, through the steaming rain forests of South America, Asia and Africa, and on to the flatlands of the Asian steppes and the mountains of Japan, there are people living lifestyles you would barely recognize, in places where you might find it hard to stay alive for more than a day. As well as struggling against difficult conditions, these peoples are trying to keep their special cultures alive.

Could you build an igloo as night began to fall, fifty miles from the nearest shelter? Would you be able to get a herd of reindeer to swim to an island where there's good grazing for them? Have you ever had to collect water for your family in the eggshell of an ostrich?

An embroidery made by a member of the Huichol in Mexico.

And what would it be like to hear that your relatives had been killed, by a cloud of poison gas released by their own government?

This book tells you about the groups who have had these experiences (the Inuit, Saami, Bushmen and Kurds) and many others besides. You can find out their way of life, their history, where they live and the difficulties they face in keeping their traditional lifestyles.

One of the biggest problems all the peoples in this book face is that they are surrounded by powerful people with a different lifestyle from their own. Often these powerful people want the land that the threatened cultures rely on; sometimes they have already taken it. In northern Canada, the Innu are finding it increasingly difficult to continue their hunting lifestyle, as

A nomadic Tuareg tribesman from North Africa.

non-Innu use their land for military activity, mining, hydroelectric stations and forestry. In Australia and New Zealand, the Aborigines and Maori are still fighting with their governments over land that was taken away from them hundreds of years ago.

A terrible danger for people who have previously lived away from others — like some of the tribes in the Amazon rain forest, who have never seen non-Amerindians before — is disease. As people from outside move into their areas, they bring with them diseases that the locals have no resistance to. Whole villages have been killed by seemingly harmless diseases such as 'flu. Many others have suffered at the hands of miners, loggers, farmers and settlers.

Yet another difficulty is that in some parts of the world people are not allowed to be different. Some governments want everyone to live in a particular way, so they make it as hard as they can for people to live a different lifestyle. Two examples of this are the Kurds, whom the Turkish government has called 'mountain Turks', refusing even to admit that the Kurds exist as a people, and the Gypsies, who in Romania have been subjected to violence, and even killed.

A warrior from one of the many groups who live on the island of New Guinea.

This book gives you information about almost a thousand different groups around the world who may find it difficult to keep their cultures alive in the twenty-first century. Some may even have disappeared by the time you have read this introduction. Many of these peoples are fighting hard to keep their cultures alive: in the back of the book are some addresses you could write to if you want to help, or to find out more.

A young Innu boy from North America.

9

THE FROZEN NORTH

All indigenous peoples in the Arctic live in countries where there is a non-indigenous majority. These populations live to the south and their governments regard the Arctic as a source of oil, gas, metals and other natural resources.

But for the many small groups of indigenous peoples who have adapted themselves over thousands of years to its extreme harshness, the Arctic is their homeland. Here, where crops cannot be grown, humans have been able to survive only by hunting large animals. The Saami and the peoples of Siberia have hunted reindeer and elk, and in recent centuries they have domesticated reindeer into large herds. In Greenland and across northern North America, the Inuit (Eskimo) peoples live along the coast, where they hunt seals, whales and walrus.

Because their food is spread out over a wide area, Arctic animals migrate huge distances. So even a tiny human population needs thousands of square kilometres to hunt and herd. The extraction of minerals and other natural resources by southern industries cuts across the animals' migration routes and pollutes the environment.

During the twentieth century, throughout the Arctic, indigenous cultures were undermined by government schemes which concentrated the scattered hunters into large villages and sent their children to grim boarding schools in distant towns. The children lost contact with their parents and with their own culture, and became incapable of hunting or living on the land. The results have been widespread despair, alcoholism and suicide. But since the 1970s, Arctic peoples have started to demand compensation for resources taken from them and for environmental damage. They have also campaigned for measures to preserve their languages and cultures.

Though they live far from big cities, Arctic peoples are seriously threatened by pollution carried in the air from the industrialized south. In Canada, Inuit women's breast milk contains high levels of mercury, while in Russia and Scandinavia huge areas have been contaminated by radioactive fall-out from nuclear explosions. But a major threat to Arctic cultures comes from some environmentalists and animal rights supporters in Europe and America. They campaign against seal hunting or whaling, without understanding the unique relationship between Arctic peoples and the animals with which they live and on which they depend to keep their cultures alive.

GIVE ME BACK MY LAND

'*The loggers even cut down all the trees on the tribal cemetery, thus ruining the final resting place. In all his 76 years, my father had not once plucked a fir needle or a leaf, not a blade of grass unnecessarily on his land, on the land of his ancestors.*

'*"What do you want, old man?" I ask my father. "Can I help you?"*

'*"I don't want anything," he says after a long silence. "Only my land. Give me back my land where I can graze my reindeer, hunt game and catch fish. Give me my land where my deer are not attacked by stray dogs and poachers, where the rivers and lakes have no oil slicks – just a patch of my own land."*

'*What can I say in reply?*'

Yeremei Aipin, a Khant writer from Siberia

A young Inuit girl wearing a hooded fox fur jacket to protect her from the extreme cold of the Arctic.

KEY TO THREATS

A Campaigns by animal rights movements/environmentalists
C Cultural breakdown/loss of language
E Environmental degradation, often through radioactive fallout/ pollution
M Christian missionaries or after-effects of communism
O Extraction of oil and gas or other minerals, timber or hydroelectric power, usually with non-recognition of traditional land rights
S Suicide/despair/alcoholism

RUSSIA
1 Chukchi — A C E M O S
2 Dolgan — C E M S
3 Entsy — C E M S
4 Eskimo (Siberian) — A C E M O S
5 Even — C E M O S
6 Evenk (Tungus) — C E M O S
7 Itelmen — C E M S
8 Ket — C E M S
9 Khant — C E M O S
10 Koryak — C E M S
11 Mansi — C E M O S
12 Nenets — C E M O S
13 Nganasan — C E M O S
14 Nivkhi — C E M O S
15 Saami — C E M S
16 Sakha (Yakut) — E M O
17 Selkup — C E M S
18 Yukaghir — C E M O S

ALASKA (USA)
19 Bering Strait Eskimo (Yuit) — A C E M S
20 North Alaskan Eskimo (Inupiat) — A C E M S

CANADA
21 Inuit — A C E M S

GREENLAND
22 Kalaallit — A C E M S

NORWAY, SWEDEN, FINLAND
23 Saami — C E M O S

Nenets

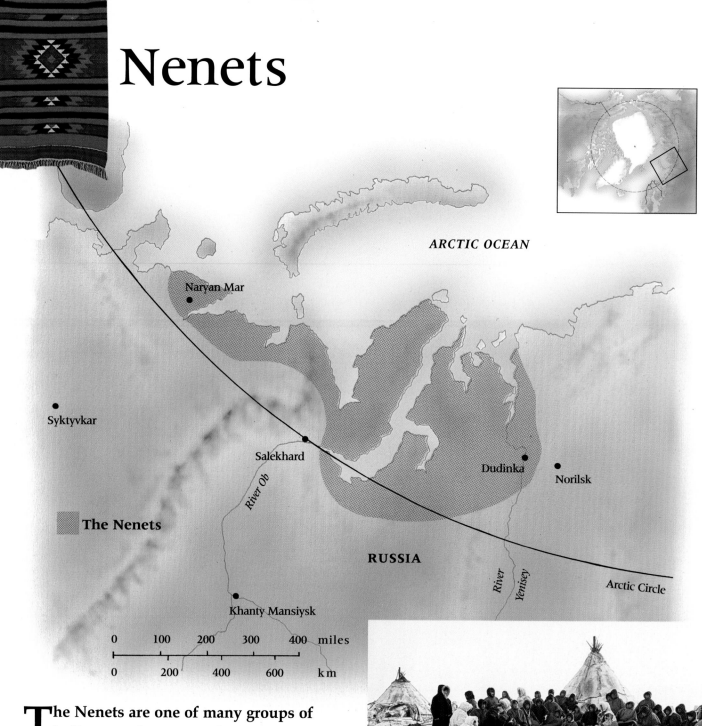

ARCTIC OCEAN

Naryan Mar

Syktyvkar

Salekhard

River Ob

The Nenets

Dudinka

Norilsk

RUSSIA

River Yenisey

Arctic Circle

Khanty Mansiysk

| 0 | 100 | 200 | 300 | 400 | miles |

| 0 | 200 | 400 | 600 | km |

The Nenets are one of many groups of indigenous hunters and reindeer herders spread thinly across the far north of Russia. In winter they move their herds of reindeer south into the forest for shelter, and in summer they move them towards the treeless coast, where the sea breezes keep the clouds of mosquitos at bay.

Gas company officials discuss gas development on Nenets land with Nenets community representatives.

Like other peoples of the Russian North, the Nenets have been weakened by three generations of Soviet Communist rule, with its attacks on the traditional clan, religion and organization of herding and hunting. Mixed marriages, Russian cultural influence and a low birth-rate have all eroded Nenets culture. But now the Nenets face an even more serious threat. Their land includes some of the world's biggest reserves of oil and natural gas, which are wanted by the cash-starved Russian state and its partners, the large multinational corporations. In the course of extraction, millions of tonnes of oil are spilled into Nenets fishing rivers, while gas pipelines hundreds of

A winter camp for a group of Nenets reindeer herders. The tents, which are made from two layers of reindeer skins, are carried on the women's sleds during migrations.

Nenets herders have caught one of their reindeer for food. A herding family may eat 80 reindeer a year.

kilometres long cut off the migration routes of their reindeer. In addition, radioactive fall-out from nuclear bomb testing during the Cold War now poisons the reindeer pastures and the reindeer meat on which the people depend, so that cancer has become a serious problem.

ALSO UNDER THREAT

Other cultures threatened by pollution and the extraction of resources in the Russian North include the Chukchi, Siberian Eskimo, Even, Evenk, Khant, Mansi, Nganasan and Yukaghir.

CELEBRATING THE ARCTIC SPRING

In spring, nomadic reindeer herders come from thousands of kilometres away to sing, dance and celebrate the end of winter. Young men compete in wrestling and reindeer racing to impress their prospective brides. Today, these festivals double as demonstrations against pollution, authoritarian government and cultural decline.

Inuit (Kalaallit)

In Greenland, the Inuit (known locally as Kalaallit) have survived for centuries along the coast by hunting seals and whales for food and clothing. Modern commodities, like medicines, snow-scooters and plane tickets, all have to be paid for out of the proceeds of hunting.

The biggest threat to Inuit culture throughout the Arctic comes from Western environmentalists and animal rights activists when they attack hunting as a way of life without understanding it. People who do not have to live off the land are destroying the culture and society of people who do. Some of these campaigns against Inuit culture have been called off, but other Western groups remain hostile.

Among all Inuit groups, the impact of missionaries and putting children in boarding schools have destroyed much of the old religion. This was based on shamans who used their helper spirits to cure illnesses. Shamans also ensured the food supply by communicating with the spirit keepers of whales and seals. Although hardly any Inuit practise the old religions, a profound respect for animals remains, since the people still have intimate contact with them and depend on hunting them for survival and for the continuation of their culture.

GREENLAND

Thule

Upernavik

Qeqertarsuaq

Ittoqqortoormiit

Arctic Circle

Angmagssalik

Nuuk

Nanortalik

0   100   200   300   miles

0   100 200 300 400 500 km

The Inuit

THE WHALE HUNT

Unlike white hunters, Inuit take only the animals they need. They say that an animal gives itself willingly in order to feed the community, and that in return the hunter must share out the meat so that no one will starve. If the hunter treats the animal with respect, the animal will offer itself to him again later when it is reborn in another body.

14

Left Inuit children help to unload mail and supplies that the helicopter has brought. The helicopter is a lifeline for small communities, and can be used as an air ambulance in an emergency.

Below An Inuit father takes his son on a hunting trip to teach him how to hunt utoq seals.

ALSO THREATENED

Other Inuit cultures threatened by Western environmental campaigners include the Bering Strait Eskimo (Yuit) and North Alaskan Eskimo (Inupiat) (Alaska, USA), the Inuit (Canada) and the Siberian Eskimo (Russia).

Left An Inuit hunter in his kayak. On the back is a seal-skin float which is attached to his harpoon.

WHAT'S IN A NAME?

There is no single word currently available for the peoples who were previously known as Eskimo. This name is still used by local people in Siberia and Alaska. But in Canada and Greenland it is considered insulting and they generally use the name Inuit, which is actually taken from the name of a Canadian group. Local groups also have their own names, like the Kalaallit in Greenland.

15

Saami

The Saami (who are sometimes called Lapps) number around 100,000 and are found throughout the north of Scandinavia and into northern Russia. Traditionally they were reindeer herders and hunters, but today only about 10 per cent of Saami follow this way of life. Others live by fishing or by the many other jobs available in modern European society.

The Saami way of life is threatened because they live so near to other Europeans. In the seventeenth century most Saami gave up their belief in spirits and shamans for Christianity, and shamans were persecuted and even killed.

LOCAL COSTUME

Saami make some of their most precious objects from reindeer antler and other local materials. Many Saami still wear their distinctive blue, red and yellow costumes on special occasions. To quote a Saami woman in Karasjok, Norway: 'You can tell exactly where anyone comes from if you know the costume. Our men have a three-pointed hat, while down in Røros the hat goes straight up and round at the top. Over in Sweden, in Karasuando, the hat is covered with a huge bobble.'

A Saami woman carries an antler that has been shed by one of the reindeer in her herd.

A Saami reindeer herder on his snow scooter. On his sled is a young reindeer too weak to migrate.

In recent years, Saami land has been used for dams, which flood reindeer pasture in order to supply hydroelectric power to cities in the south. Radiation from the Chernobyl nuclear disaster in far-off Ukraine has poisoned the reindeer pasture. Tourists from the south pick the Saami's berries, shoot their game animals and gaze at the people as quaint curiosities. For a long time, the Saami language was not taught in schools and Saami were made to speak Norwegian, Swedish, Finnish or Russian and to feel ashamed of their identity.

But the Saami are now becoming more confident about their own identity. They have fought against dam-building projects, their language is being taught in schools and there is a revived interest in Saami history.

Above right **A big problem for Saami reindeer herders is nasal warbles – the larvae of the warble fly. This reindeer calf had so many larvae growing in its throat that it was suffocated by them. The problem is partly caused by the fact that the pastures are being grazed by too many reindeer, which concentrates the parasites. The reindeer are starving and, in their weakened state, have less resistance to infection.**

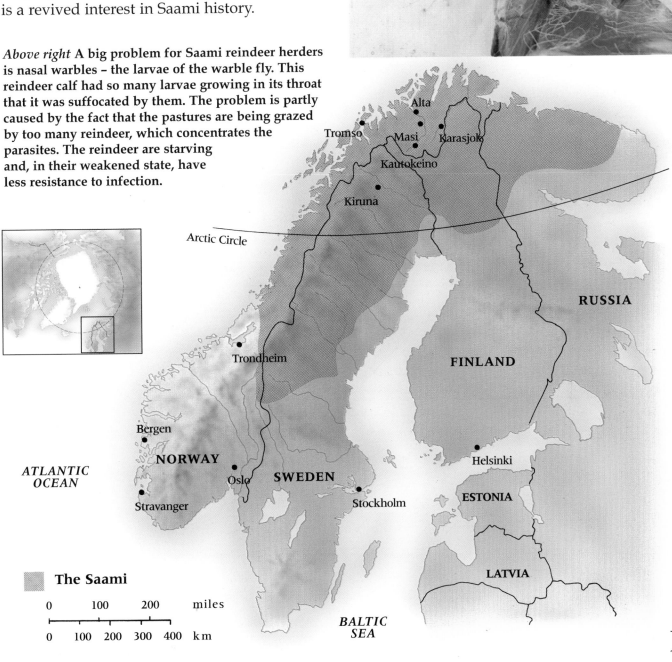

ATLANTIC
OCEAN

The Saami

| 0 | 100 | 200 | miles |

| 0 | 100 | 200 | 300 | 400 | k m |

NORTH AMERICA

There are around three million Native North Americans living in Canada and the United States today. They belong to hundreds of different tribes and nations, ranging from the Navajo, with a population of about 230,000 and a homeland as large as the country of Belgium, to very small communities with only a handful of members and a few acres of land.

Native American cultures and ways of life vary greatly. Some groups continue to speak their own languages and to follow a traditional lifestyle, while others now live much like their non-native neighbours. More than half of all Native Americans live and work in cities, away from their own communities, although often they intend to return home when they retire.

Like the Amerindians of South America, Native North Americans are thought to be descended from Ice Age hunters who crossed from Asia to Alaska more than 20,000 years ago.

By the time Columbus 'discovered' America in 1492, Native Americans had evolved into many distinct peoples, ranging from small nomadic hunting groups in the far north to large farming nations in what is now the southern United States. Each group was closely adapted to its own area, and felt a deep attachment to the land and to the plants and animals with which they shared it.

The arrival of Europeans was a disaster for Native North Americans. Millions were killed or displaced by settlers, who saw them as savages with no right to the land. Millions more died from European diseases against which they had no resistance. By the end of the nineteenth century, the native peoples had lost almost all their land, and their population had fallen from an estimated six million or more to only 350,000.

Today, Native North Americans are no longer being deliberately killed by the Canadian and US governments. Nonetheless, they still have a great many problems to contend with.

THE BLESSINGS OF THE GREAT MYSTERY

'We did not think of the great open plains, the beautiful rolling hills, and winding streams with tangled growth as "wild". Only to the white man was nature a "wilderness" and only to him was the land "infested" with "wild" animals and "savage" people. To us it was tame. Earth was bountiful and we were surrounded with the blessings of the Great Mystery. Not until the hairy man from the east came and with brutal frenzy heaped injustices upon us and the families we loved, was it "wild" for us. When the very animals of the forest began fleeing from his approach, then it was that for us the "Wild West" began.'

Luther Standing Bear, Sioux

An elderly Hopi woman.

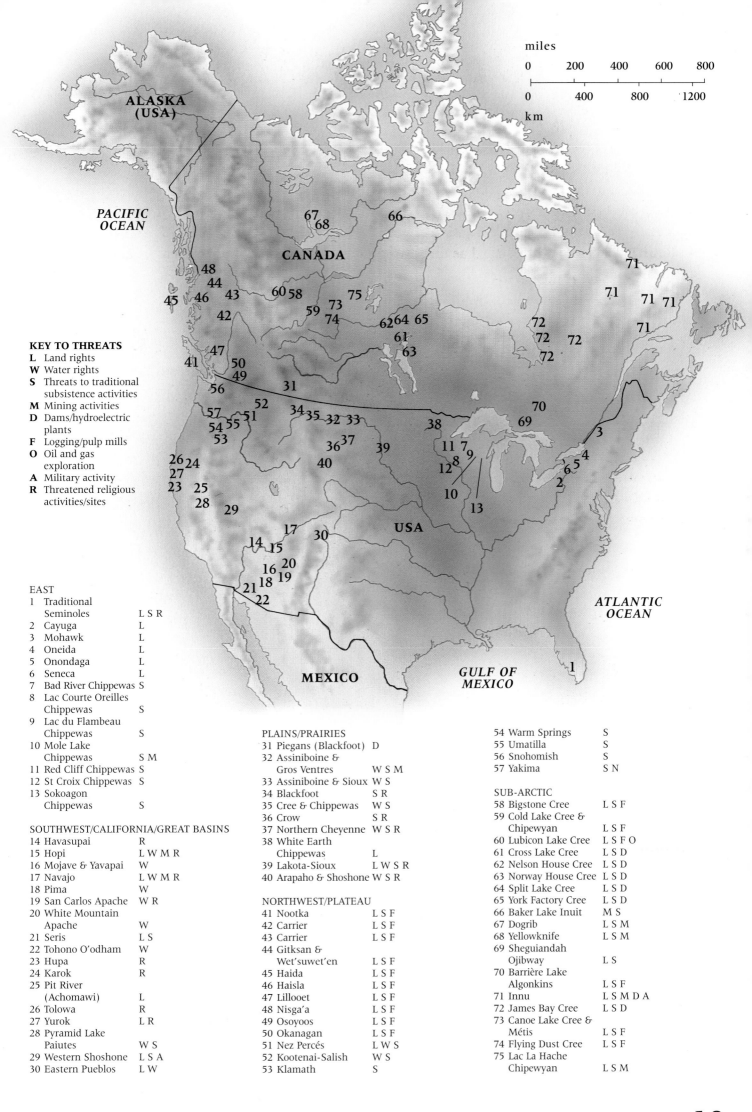

ALASKA
(USA)

PACIFIC
OCEAN

CANADA

miles
0   200   400   600   800

0   400   800   1200
km

KEY TO THREATS
L Land rights
W Water rights
S Threats to traditional
   subsistence activities
M Mining activities
D Dams/hydroelectric
   plants
F Logging/pulp mills
O Oil and gas
   exploration
A Military activity
R Threatened religious
   activities/sites

USA

MEXICO

GULF OF
MEXICO

ATLANTIC
OCEAN

EAST
1	Traditional Seminoles	L S R
2	Cayuga	L
3	Mohawk	L
4	Oneida	L
5	Onondaga	L
6	Seneca	L
7	Bad River Chippewas	S
8	Lac Courte Oreilles Chippewas	S
9	Lac du Flambeau Chippewas	S
10	Mole Lake Chippewas	S M
11	Red Cliff Chippewas	S
12	St Croix Chippewas	S
13	Sokoagon Chippewas	S

SOUTHWEST/CALIFORNIA/GREAT BASINS
14	Havasupai	R
15	Hopi	L W M R
16	Mojave & Yavapai	W
17	Navajo	L W M R
18	Pima	W
19	San Carlos Apache	W R
20	White Mountain Apache	W
21	Seris	L S
22	Tohono O'odham	W
23	Hupa	R
24	Karok	R
25	Pit River (Achomawi)	L
26	Tolowa	R
27	Yurok	L R
28	Pyramid Lake Paiutes	W S
29	Western Shoshone	L S A
30	Eastern Pueblos	L W

PLAINS/PRAIRIES
31	Piegans (Blackfoot)	D
32	Assiniboine & Gros Ventres	W S M
33	Assiniboine & Sioux	W S
34	Blackfoot	S R
35	Cree & Chippewas	W S
36	Crow	S R
37	Northern Cheyenne	W S R
38	White Earth Chippewas	L
39	Lakota-Sioux	L W S R
40	Arapaho & Shoshone	W S R

NORTHWEST/PLATEAU
41	Nootka	L S F
42	Carrier	L S F
43	Carrier	L S F
44	Gitksan & Wet'suwet'en	L S F
45	Haida	L S F
46	Haisla	L S F
47	Lillooet	L S F
48	Nisga'a	L S F
49	Osoyoos	L S F
50	Okanagan	L S F
51	Nez Percés	L W S
52	Kootenai-Salish	W S
53	Klamath	S

54	Warm Springs	S
55	Umatilla	S
56	Snohomish	S
57	Yakima	S N

SUB-ARCTIC
58	Bigstone Cree	L S F
59	Cold Lake Cree & Chipewyan	L S F
60	Lubicon Lake Cree	L S F O
61	Cross Lake Cree	L S D
62	Nelson House Cree	L S D
63	Norway House Cree	L S D
64	Split Lake Cree	L S D
65	York Factory Cree	L S D
66	Baker Lake Inuit	M S
67	Dogrib	L S M
68	Yellowknife	L S M
69	Sheguiandah Ojibway	L S
70	Barrière Lake Algonkins	L S F
71	Innu	L S M D A
72	James Bay Cree	L S D
73	Canoe Lake Cree & Métis	L S F
74	Flying Dust Cree	L S F
75	Lac La Hache Chipewyan	L S M

19

NORTH AMERICA (cont.)

Much of the remaining Native American land in the United States and southern Canada is affected by water shortage, pollution, mining, military activity or the growth of nearby non-native communities. Some tribes face threats to traditional activities such as hunting, fishing and food gathering. Many groups are trying to regain land that was taken from them illegally, or to prevent the destruction of important sacred sites, which are essential to their religion.

Further north, in northern Canada and Alaska, peoples such as the Innu and the Cree are facing an invasion of their homeland. Until recently, this vast area of lakes, forests and tundra had attracted few settlers, and the indigenous people could hunt, fish and trap like their ancestors. Although many groups have never signed treaties giving up their land, they are now threatened by many kinds of development: military training, diamond and uranium mining, oil and gas extraction, and hydroelectric projects, such as the enormous James Bay scheme in Quebec. Perhaps most devastating of all, multinational companies are clear-cutting the forests of northern Canada at the rate of one hectare every 30 seconds, causing immense environmental damage and destroying the indigenous people's way of life.

Some Native North American groups have successfully adapted aspects of their own culture to help them survive. In the Southwest, for instance, many tribes sell pottery and other traditional handicrafts to tourists. A few have developed new activities, such as tourism and mining. Most, however, are plagued by poverty, unemployment and disease. They are also threatened by intense pressure, particularly from television and the educational system, to assimilate into mainstream North American society. This leaves many indigenous people demoralized and confused, and contributes to the high rates of alcoholism, suicide and social problems in their communities.

A group of young Native American children in Albuquerque, New Mexico, dressed up for a dance.

RESPECT FOR THE LAND

'This land, these forests, are not just a resource to be harvested and managed. They were given to us to take care of and treat with respect, the way our grandfathers have always done. We are responsible for taking care of Mother Earth because Mother Earth takes care of us... We have lived with this land for many generations. We know its cycles. We know it won't be the same after they take away the trees. The money is all that will be left.'

Bigstone Cree First Nation, Canada

Innu

The 13,000 Innu (not to be confused with their neighbours the Inuit, or Eskimo) are the indigenous people of a large area in north-eastern Canada. Their homeland, which they call *Nitassinan*, is a vast expanse of forests, lakes and rocky, windswept 'barrens'. For most of the year it lies under a deep blanket of snow and ice.

The Innu survived here for thousands of years by hunting caribou and other animals. From September to June, small bands of perhaps two or three families would travel in search of game, walking on snowshoes and pushing their possessions on a sled. Then during the summer, the Innu would come together in larger groups at the coast to fish, make boats and meet friends and relatives.

Since the 1950s, their way of life has been coming under increasing pressure. The authorities have discouraged the Innu from hunting and tried to make them settle in permanent villages and send their children to school to become 'Canadians'. Many Innu have become confused and demoralized, and their communities are plagued by alcoholism, family breakdown and suicide. In one village, in 1993, a third of the adults tried to kill themselves.

At the same time the Innu's land, which they have never sold or surrendered to Canada, is seriously threatened by modern development. Hydroelectric and forestry projects are destroying or damaging thousands of square kilometres. The Canadian government is also using *Nitassinan* as a training ground for military pilots. Low-level jets fly at supersonic speeds close to the ground, terrifying the Innu and disrupting wildlife.

Perhaps most seriously, the discovery of mineral deposits at Voysey's Bay on the Labrador coast threatens to bring thousands of miners flooding into the area. If that happens, according to one Innu leader, 'It will mean the death of my people.'

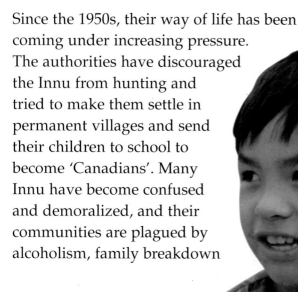

ALSO THREATENED

Other groups threatened by development of their lands include the Gitksan, Wet'suwet'en, Nisga'a, Lubicon Lake Cree, Sheguiandah Ojibway, Barrière Lake Algonkins and James Bay Cree.

A young Innu boy with freshly caught lake trout, or *kokomis*.

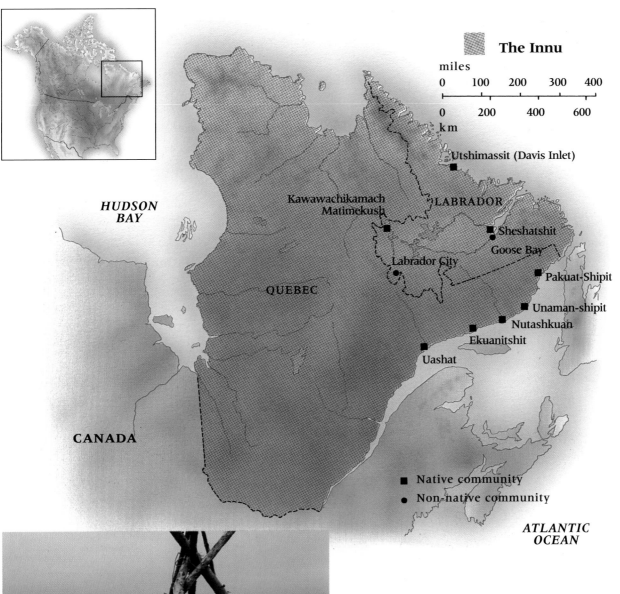

The Innu

miles
0   100   200   300   400

0   200   400   600
km

Utshimassit (Davis Inlet)

HUDSON
BAY

Kawawachikamach
Matimekush
LABRADOR

Sheshatshit

Goose Bay

Labrador City

Pakuat-Shipit

QUEBEC

Unaman-shipit

Nutashkuan

Ekuanitshit

Uashat

CANADA

■ Native community
● Non-native community

ATLANTIC
OCEAN

An Innu woman at a hunting camp, drying meat to store. A traditional rack of branches has been erected with a fire in the centre to smoke the meat.

ANIMAL MASTERS

The Innu believe that the animals they hunt are controlled by spiritual 'masters', who help the Innu to find and kill game. In return, they must show respect to the masters by following certain rituals and sharing the meat among themselves.

The most important ritual is *Mukushan*. A sacred food is prepared from the bone marrow of the caribou, and then everyone in the camp is invited to eat it at a special meal. It is essential that every scrap should be eaten, otherwise the 'master' may be angry and prevent them from killing more caribou.

Haisla

Two Haisla people with their catch of salmon.

This way of life was devastated when British colonists started to arrive in the nineteenth century. Settlers seized indigenous lands, missionaries suppressed 'heathen' practices like the *potlatch*, and European diseases killed tens of thousands of native people. As late as 1949, the Haisla were almost exterminated by an outbreak of influenza. Today, their community suffers from 60 per cent unemployment and acute social problems.

Since the mid-1980s, the Haisla have faced another threat. Logging companies want to cut down the *Kitlope*, a 400,000 hectare forest where Haisla have hunted and fished for 3,000 years. Pulp mills have been built to process the timber that is cut down, and these mills have caused pollution of the rivers in the area. Tribal elders, believing that it will mean the end of their culture, have campaigned against the logging. In 1994, the government agreed to protect the *Kitlope*, but it remains to be seen if the Haisla's victory is permanent.

The 600 Haisla live in British Columbia, a lush, temperate area of dense forests and teeming rivers. The Haisla and their neighbours used this natural abundance to create a unique culture. They hunted deer, gathered berries and – most importantly – harvested the millions of salmon that swarmed through their rivers every spring. The surplus catch was smoked or dried to provide food for the rest of the year.

West-coast peoples had a rich artistic and social life. One of their most important celebrations was the *potlatch*. This was a ritual feast in which wealthy individuals gave away food and possessions, believing – in the words of a modern West-coast Canadian – that 'the more you give, the richer you are.'

ALSO THREATENED

Other Native North American groups threatened by forestry include the Nootka, Bigstone Cree, Barrière Lake Algonkins, Carrier, Cold Lake Cree and Chipewyan, Haida, Canoe Lake Cree and Métis, Lillooet, Lubicon Lake Cree, Osoyoos, Flying Dust Cree and Okanagan.

All the trees in this area of forest have been cut down by logging companies.

These brightly painted totem poles are in Vancouver, Canada. Although they have been placed there as a tourist attraction, they show the art of a very famous Native American tradition.

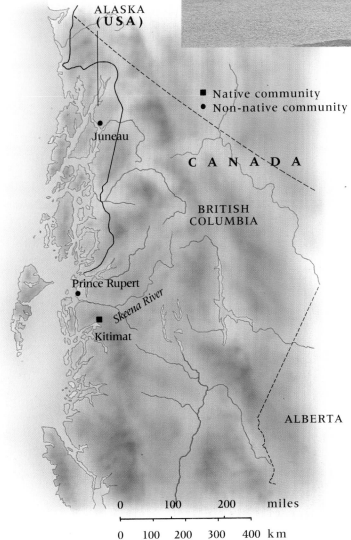

ALASKA
(USA)

Native community
Non-native community

Juneau

C A N A D A

BRITISH
COLUMBIA

Prince Rupert

Skeena River

Kitimat

ALBERTA

0   100   200   miles

0   100   200   300   400 k m

TOTEM POLES

North-west coast peoples have always been superb artists. They wove beautiful clothes and blankets from shredded cedar bark, and carved intricate, brilliantly coloured masks used by dancers in the many festivals and ceremonies during the year. Most famously, they produced enormous, brightly painted totem poles.

A totem pole was really a kind of family tree that stood in front of the owner's house. Often it shows not only human ancestors but also powerful animals like the raven and the wolf and mythical beings, such as the thunderbird, from which important families believed they were descended. A few outstanding native artists are still carving in the traditional way today.

Traditional Seminoles

The 200 or so Traditional Seminoles live in the dense, subtropical Florida Everglades, one of the last wildernesses in eastern North America. They are almost unique, still building their own straw-thatched houses, or *chickees*, and following a way of life based on hunting and fishing.

Although the US signed an agreement recognizing the Traditional Seminoles' land rights in 1842, almost all their territory has since been seized by settlers or destroyed by development. The Traditional Seminoles are now reduced to being little more than squatters in their own homeland.

Recently, the US government has offered them millions of dollars in compensation for the loss of their lands. Although they are desperately poor, the Traditional Seminoles – unlike most other tribes – have refused. They explain: 'The Great Spirit put the land here… We don't believe in accepting money for the land because the land is not ours to sell.' If the government does not respect their right to live and use the land traditionally, they fear that they – and the Everglades they have protected for so long – may not survive.

THE GREEN CORN DANCE

For the Traditional Seminoles and the other indigenous peoples of the south-east, the Green Corn Dance is the most important festival of the year. Under the guidance of a shaman (or medicine man), they gather for five days to celebrate and renew their life as a people through ceremonies, rituals and meetings.

Danny Billie, a Traditional Seminole leader, says: 'The Green Corn Dance defines who we are and what we are… It is the heart and soul of our way of life.' The Traditional Seminoles are now trying to find a permanent site for the Dance so that their culture can continue.

Danny Billie, a Traditional Seminole leader, reads a notice posted on agricultural land. The land was granted to the Traditional Seminoles over 150 years ago but was then taken by settlers.

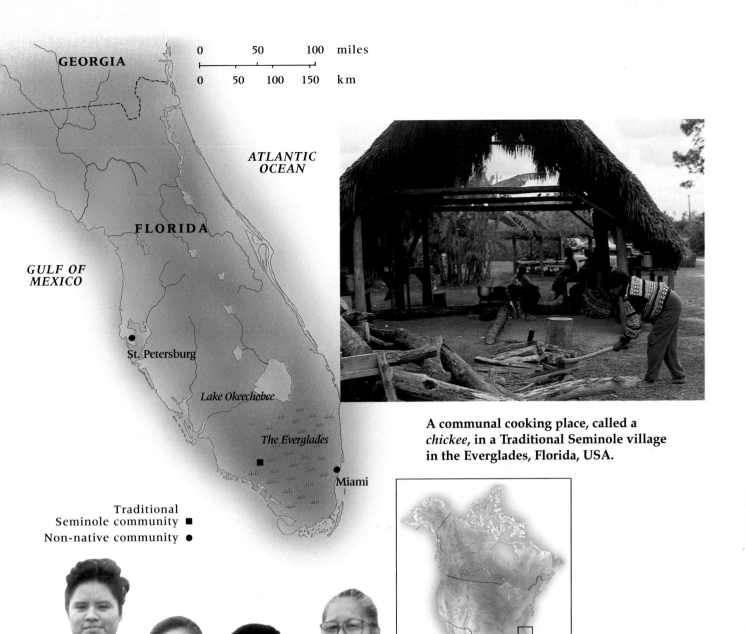

GEORGIA

0   50   100   miles

0   50   100   150   km

ATLANTIC
OCEAN

FLORIDA

GULF OF
MEXICO

St. Petersburg

Lake Okeechobee

The Everglades

Miami

Traditional
Seminole community ■
Non-native community ●

A communal cooking place, called a *chickee*, in a Traditional Seminole village in the Everglades, Florida, USA.

ALSO UNDER THREAT

Other Native North American groups trying to regain lost land include the Cayuga, Seris, Mohawk, Pit River (Achomawi), Oneida, Western Shoshones, Onondaga, Lakota-Sioux and Seneca.

Three generations of Traditional Seminole women and children in traditional costume.

27

Sioux

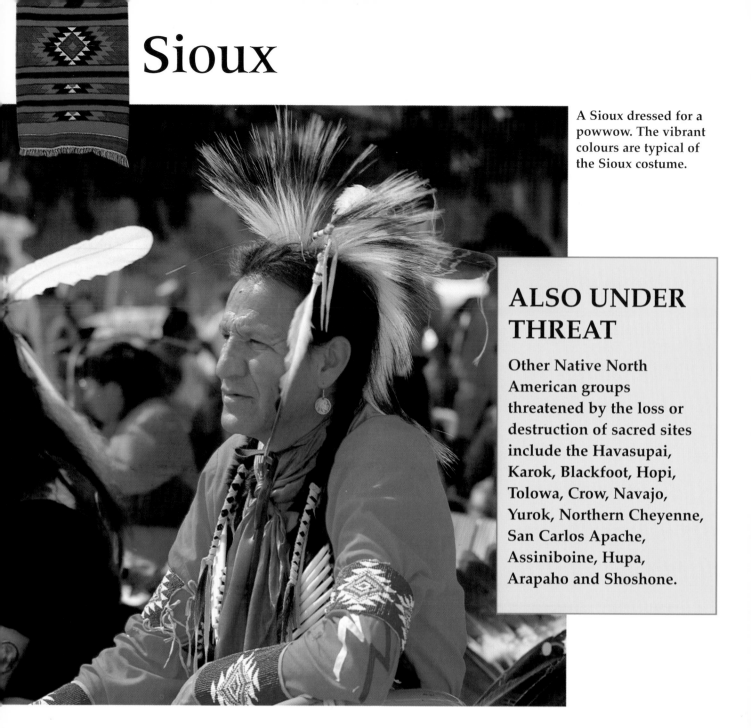

A Sioux dressed for a powwow. The vibrant colours are typical of the Sioux costume.

ALSO UNDER THREAT

Other Native North American groups threatened by the loss or destruction of sacred sites include the Havasupai, Karok, Blackfoot, Hopi, Tolowa, Crow, Navajo, Yurok, Northern Cheyenne, San Carlos Apache, Assiniboine, Hupa, Arapaho and Shoshone.

The Sioux are one of the largest and best-known of all Native American groups. More than any other people, they represent what is often seen as the 'typical Indian': the mounted warrior wearing a feather war bonnet, living in a tepee and hunting bison on the windswept grasslands of the Great Plains.

During the nineteenth century, the Sioux and their neighbouring groups fought heroically against overwhelming odds to protect this way of life. Eventually, though, the United States defeated them by deliberately hunting the bison on which the Sioux depended to the edge of extinction.

Today, most Sioux live on reservations, but conditions are so bad there that many of them – like other Native Americans – are moving to the cities. The reservations are among the poorest communities in North America, with very high rates of unemployment, disease, drunkenness, suicide and accidental death.

The Sioux are trying to rebuild their pride and identity as a people. In particular, they want the United States to return *Paha Sapa*, the Black Hills, which were taken from them illegally in the 1870s. They have refused compensation of more than $100 million because they believe these hills are the sacred centre of the universe, 'The Heart of Everything that Is.'

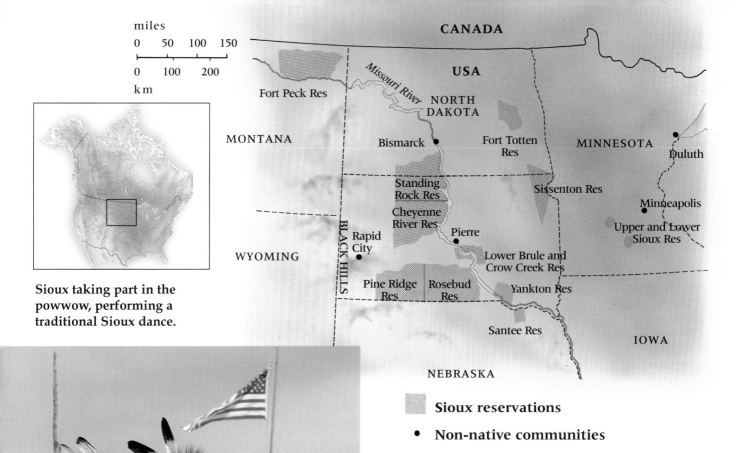

miles

| 0 | 50 | 100 | 150 |

| 0 | 100 | 200 |

km

CANADA

USA

Missouri River

NORTH DAKOTA

Fort Peck Res

MONTANA

Bismarck

Fort Totten Res

MINNESOTA

Duluth

Standing Rock Res

Sissenton Res

Cheyenne River Res

Minneapolis

Pierre

Upper and Lower Sioux Res

Rapid City

WYOMING

BLACK HILLS

Lower Brule and Crow Creek Res

Pine Ridge Res

Rosebud Res

Yankton Res

Santee Res

IOWA

NEBRASKA

Sioux taking part in the powwow, performing a traditional Sioux dance.

▨ Sioux reservations

• Non-native communities

POWWOWS

Every summer, there are hundreds of powwows in Native American communities. For three days, dancers in brilliantly coloured headdresses and costumes perform, accompanied by singing and drumming. People have a chance to meet friends and relatives from different reservations and to enjoy traditional foods and customs.

Mining, tourism and other developments have already damaged *Paha Sapa*. Now the film star Kevin Costner wants to build a giant gambling and leisure complex there.

'We have a prophecy,' says a modern Sioux, Charlotte Black Elk, 'that 112 years after humans drive the last bear from the Black Hills, there will come a day of great, catastrophic change. So far as we know, there hasn't been a bear there since the end of the 1880s. That doesn't give us long to get the Hills back and return the bear to them.'

Pine Ridge Reservation, one of the Sioux reservations, in South Dakota.

The Hopi

The Hopi live in the hot, arid region of Arizona in the south-western United States. They are the most westerly of the Pueblo peoples, desert farmers who build hill-top villages of tightly packed adobe houses, and irrigate the land to grow maize, squash, beans and other crops. Their life follows the cycle of the seasons, with spectacular festivals marking important times of the year such as the start of spring. During these ceremonies, which can last for days at a time, the central square of each village fills with elaborately dressed *kachinas*, messengers between the people and their gods and ancestors.

Despite the impact of Spanish and American settlers and missionaries, Hopi culture has, remarkably, survived. Today, however, it faces increasing encroachment from the outside world. The nearby Black Mesa coal mine threatens the underground water supply on which the tribe's desert farming depends. Traditional Hopi feel that the mine itself is sacrilegious, endangering not only their own culture but the whole world. As a group of elders put it, 'Hopi land is held in trust in a spiritual way for the Great Spirit, Massau'u… The area we call "Tukunavi" [which includes Black Mesa] is part of the heart of our Mother Earth… The land is sacred and if the land is abused, the sacredness of Hopi life will disappear and all other life as well.'

Two Hopi men performing the Eagle Dance at the Grand Canyon, Arizona, USA.

ALSO UNDER THREAT

Other Native North American groups threatened by water rights problems include the Mojave, Yavapai, Nez Percés, Assiniboine, Sioux, Navajo, Pyramid Lake Paiutes, Pima, Cree, Chippewa, White Mountain Apache, Eastern Pueblos, Northern Cheyenne, Tohono O'odham, Gros Ventres and Lakota.

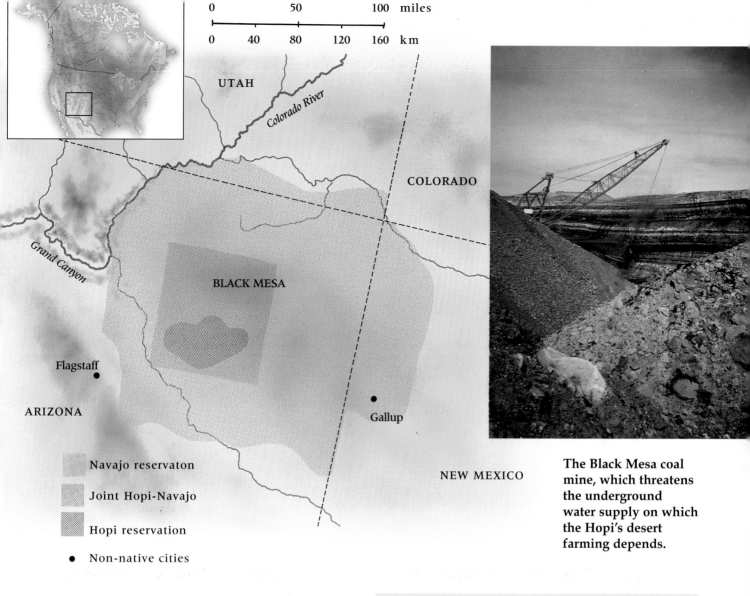

The Black Mesa coal mine, which threatens the underground water supply on which the Hopi's desert farming depends.

A typical Hopi house in a hill-top village. It is built of adobe – sun-dried mud bricks.

PUEBLO HOUSES

Many Hopi and other Pueblo people still live in traditional flat-roofed adobe (mud) or stone houses. For reasons of defence, Pueblo villages are generally built high on mesas (flat-topped hills). The houses are arranged around large plazas, where dances and celebrations are held, and underground *kivas*, which are used for religious ceremonies.

exico and the seven countries that make up Central America are the home of 15 million indigenous people. Mexico has the most indigenous cultures: 55, each with its own language. There, the descendants of the great pre-Columbian civilizations of the Mayas and Aztecs still keep much of their traditional culture. Nahuatl, the Aztec language, is today spoken by five million Indians. Many Mayan groups still live on the lands of their ancestors in southern Mexico and large parts of Guatemala, Belize, El Salvador and Honduras.

Geographically speaking, Central America and Mexico are usually regarded as being part of the North American continent. However, the peoples who live there are ethnically, culturally and historically closer to each other than they are to the groups living in the USA and Canada.

The effects of 500 years of colonization and subsequent conflicts, loss of lands and introduced diseases have left indigenous Central American peoples spread unevenly. While only 1 per cent of Costa Rica's population, for example, is indigenous, at least half of all Guatemalans belong to indigenous – mostly Mayan – groups.

NO ONE IS BETTER THAN THE REST

'We want our rights as peoples acknowledged and respected. So far a few individuals have been accepted but not our ideas, which is why we have to keep working. Sometimes it is hard to accept, but amongst us Maya no one is better than the rest, or is worth more than the rest: we are all equals. Sometimes those who have been educated do not understand what we, who have not been to school, can say in our simple words.'

Perspectivas y Propuestas de los Pueblos Mayas de Guatemala, (Views and proposals of the Maya People of Guatemala), Fundación Vicente Menchú, 1994.

These K'iche' Maya, dressed in traditional costume, are members of a *cofradia*, a religious brotherhood that looks after one or more saints in the Catholic church in their village. The men are holding their staffs of office, called *escudos*. Many *cofradia* are threatened by lack of money or by their members being converted by US evangelical sects.

During the twentieth century, the worst threats to the peoples of Central America came from decades of military dictatorships and government repression, causing serious violations of human rights.

Mayan peoples, especially, faced intensive military repression. In Guatemala, where a war was fought during the 1970s and 1980s against a poor people's army, military governments tried to eliminate as many Indians as possible. The government claimed the Indians sympathized with the rebels. Indians in Guatemala today are still being killed, despite the country's return to democratic government.

In El Salvador and Nicaragua, indigenous peoples have also been caught up in recurring civil wars, with many killed or forcibly removed from their homes. In the Mexican state of Chiapas, Mayan peoples have suffered in a civil war that began in January 1994 between a left-wing political movement (the Zapatistas) and the army, over rights of poor farmers to their land. Many Mexican Indians who have campaigned for the return of their lands or for self-determination have mysteriously 'disappeared'.

Land disputes continue to be a major problem in Central America. Indian lands are taken for ranching, logging or development projects. Huge numbers of Indians have been turned into landless peasants and forced into slums. In general they face racism and discrimination and are struggling for the recognition of their most basic rights.

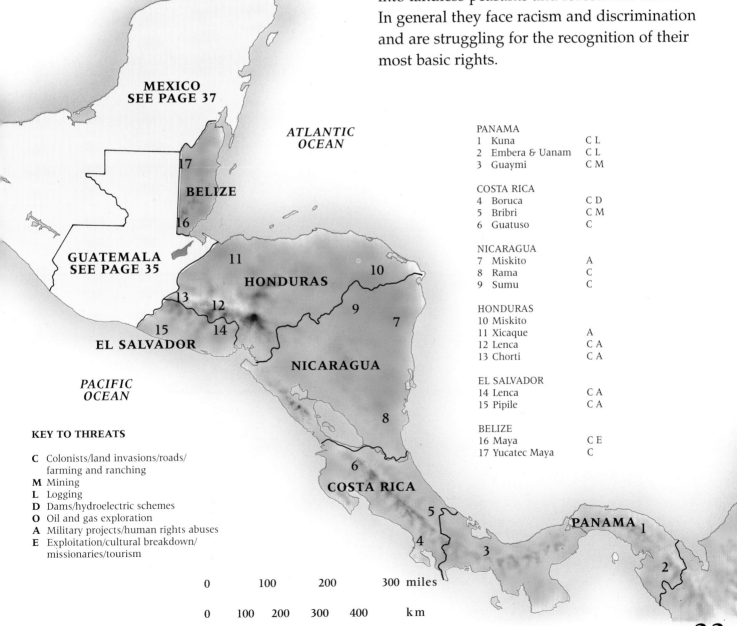

MEXICO
SEE PAGE 37

ATLANTIC
OCEAN

BELIZE

GUATEMALA
SEE PAGE 35

HONDURAS

EL SALVADOR

NICARAGUA

PACIFIC
OCEAN

COSTA RICA

PANAMA

KEY TO THREATS

C Colonists/land invasions/roads/
   farming and ranching
M Mining
L Logging
D Dams/hydroelectric schemes
O Oil and gas exploration
A Military projects/human rights abuses
E Exploitation/cultural breakdown/
   missionaries/tourism

PANAMA
1 Kuna   C L
2 Embera & Uanam   C L
3 Guaymi   C M

COSTA RICA
4 Boruca   C D
5 Bribri   C M
6 Guatuso   C

NICARAGUA
7 Miskito   A
8 Rama   C
9 Sumu   C

HONDURAS
10 Miskito
11 Xicaque   A
12 Lenca   C A
13 Chorti   C A

EL SALVADOR
14 Lenca   C A
15 Pipile   C A

BELIZE
16 Maya   C E
17 Yucatec Maya   C

0   100   200   300 miles

0   100   200   300   400   k m

The K'iche' Maya

The K'iche' are one of the 23 Mayan peoples of Guatemala who have their own language and customs. They live in the mountains in the province of El Quiché in the south-east of the country. Like other Guatemalan Mayans today, most are now poor farmers. Each family has its own tiny plot of land (a *milpa*) where maize and beans are grown. Maize is the Mayans' staple food and is made into *tortillas* (flat pancakes) that are eaten at every meal.

A young K'iche' Maya girl in the brightly coloured clothes typical of her people.

K'iche' Maya women in their vibrant dresses at the market, buying and selling their produce.

Since Guatemalan independence from Spain in 1839, the Mayans have been forced by the government to give up more and more of their land. Much of this has been used for coffee plantations owned by a few rich families. For eight months every year, K'iche' Mayan families are forced to work on the cotton or sugar cane plantations on the coast, or picking coffee, for hardly any pay.

Because the Mayans protested about the loss of their land and their cruel treatment by the government, the Guatemalan army has been torturing and killing them. El Quiché is one of the areas that has suffered most. People who stand up for their rights are still being murdered and the parents of over 5,000 children have been killed.

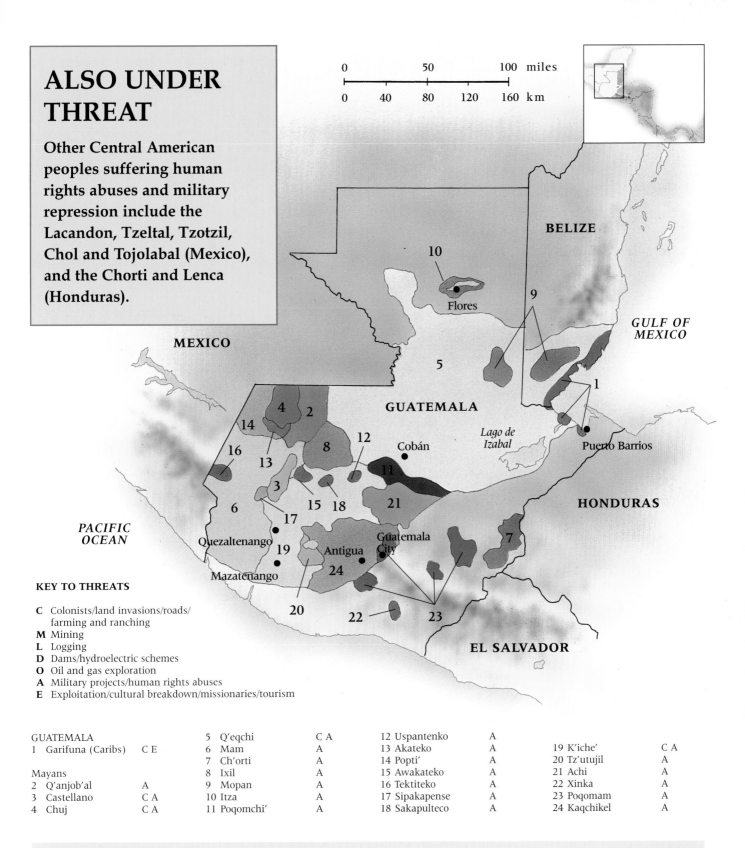

ALSO UNDER THREAT

Other Central American peoples suffering human rights abuses and military repression include the Lacandon, Tzeltal, Tzotzil, Chol and Tojolabal (Mexico), and the Chorti and Lenca (Honduras).

BELIZE

GULF OF MEXICO

MEXICO

10
Flores

9

5

GUATEMALA

4   2

14

16   13   8   12

Cobán

11

Lago de Izabal

1

Puerto Barrios

15   18

3

6   17   21

HONDURAS

PACIFIC OCEAN

Quezaltenango   19

Guatemala City

Antigua

7

Mazatenango   24

20   22   23

EL SALVADOR

KEY TO THREATS

C Colonists/land invasions/roads/
   farming and ranching
M Mining
L Logging
D Dams/hydroelectric schemes
O Oil and gas exploration
A Military projects/human rights abuses
E Exploitation/cultural breakdown/missionaries/tourism

GUATEMALA								
1 Garifuna (Caribs)	C E	5 Q'eqchi	C A	12 Uspantenko	A			
		6 Mam	A	13 Akateko	A	19 K'iche'	C A	
Mayans		7 Ch'orti	A	14 Popti'	A	20 Tz'utujil	A	
2 Q'anjob'al	A	8 Ixil	A	15 Awakateko	A	21 Achi	A	
3 Castellano	C A	9 Mopan	A	16 Tektiteko	A	22 Xinka	A	
4 Chuj	C A	10 Itza	A	17 Sipakapense	A	23 Poqomam	A	
		11 Poqomchi'	A	18 Sakapulteco	A	24 Kaqchikel	A	

NOBEL PEACE PRIZE

Rigoberta Menchú is a K'iche' Mayan woman from Guatemala. On 16 October 1992, she was awarded the Nobel Peace Prize for speaking out against the savage and persistent oppression of her people by the Guatemalan army.

From 1960-95, the Guatemalan government killed 150,000 Indians. This was the biggest massacre of Indians anywhere in the Americas in the twentieth century. Between 1978 and 1985, 440 villages were destroyed and about one million people were forced from their homes. Of these, 500,000 fled to Mexico and other neighbouring countries.

The Huichol

The Huichol live in the rugged mountains of the Western Sierra Madre in the north of the state of Jalisco, Mexico. Although they interact with Westerners in a number of ways, they are considered to be among the Mexican peoples whose culture has been least affected by Western culture.

The beliefs of the Huichol go back thousands of years. At the centre of their religious beliefs are personalized forces of nature, including *Tatewari* (Fire), *Nakawe* (Fertility) and *Kayaumari* (the Deer). The deer is very important to them, and before certain rituals men often go on a deer hunt. Huichol shamans (*maracames*), contact the spirit world by eating the sacred cactus, peyote.

The Huichol cultivate maize, beans and pumpkins, but they also raise cows and sheep, some of which they sell. Pottery, weavings and jewellery are also sold to raise money. Some people take poorly paid jobs in other areas.

With the help of expensive lawyers and friends in the government, Mexican cattle ranchers are trying to take what little remains of Huichol land. In many areas the Huichol now suffer from malnutrition and introduced diseases, and are shot at by ranchers.

Above **The Huichol agricultural year is marked out by religious festivals. This procession in San Andres Cohamiata, Jalisco, is to celebrate the end of the dry season.**

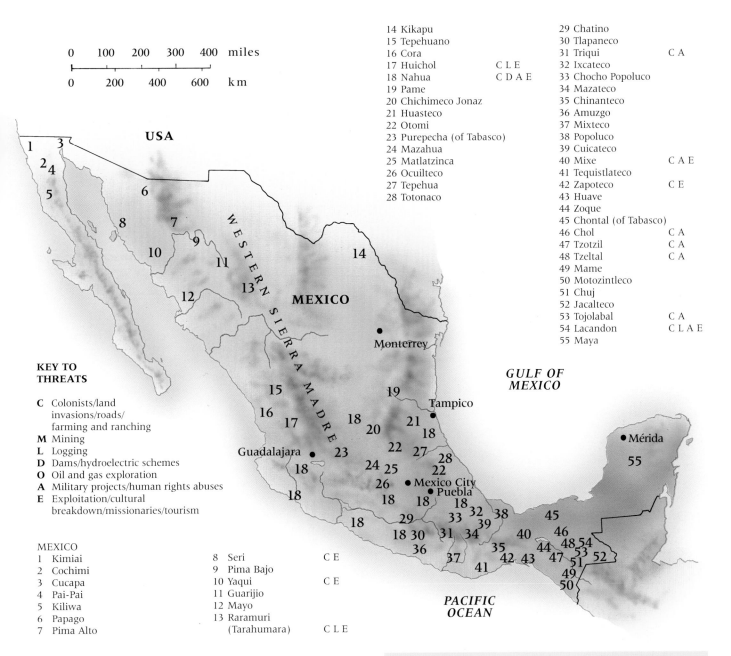

0 100 200 300 400 miles

0 200 400 600 k m

USA

MEXICO

WESTERN SIERRA MADRE

Monterrey

GULF OF MEXICO

Tampico

Guadalajara

Mérida

Mexico City
Puebla

PACIFIC OCEAN

14 Kikapu
15 Tepehuano
16 Cora
17 Huichol   C L E
18 Nahua   C D A E
19 Pame
20 Chichimeco Jonaz
21 Huasteco
22 Otomi
23 Purepecha (of Tabasco)
24 Mazahua
25 Matlatzinca
26 Ocuilteco
27 Tepehua
28 Totonaco

29 Chatino
30 Tlapaneco
31 Triqui   C A
32 Ixcateco
33 Chocho Popoluco
34 Mazateco
35 Chinanteco
36 Amuzgo
37 Mixteco
38 Popoluco
39 Cuicateco
40 Mixe   C A E
41 Tequistlateco
42 Zapoteco   C E
43 Huave
44 Zoque
45 Chontal (of Tabasco)
46 Chol   C A
47 Tzotzil   C A
48 Tzeltal   C A
49 Mame
50 Motozintleco
51 Chuj
52 Jacalteco
53 Tojolabal   C A
54 Lacandon   C L A E
55 Maya

KEY TO THREATS

C   Colonists/land invasions/roads/ farming and ranching
M   Mining
L   Logging
D   Dams/hydroelectric schemes
O   Oil and gas exploration
A   Military projects/human rights abuses
E   Exploitation/cultural breakdown/missionaries/tourism

MEXICO
1   Kimiai
2   Cochimi
3   Cucapa
4   Pai-Pai
5   Kiliwa
6   Papago
7   Pima Alto

8   Seri   C E
9   Pima Bajo
10   Yaqui   C E
11   Guarijio
12   Mayo
13   Raramuri (Tarahumara)   C L E

Inset left This picture, consisting of complex symbols embroidered in brightly coloured yarns, shows myths and ceremonies of the Huichol. Father Sun attends a ceremony held in his honour by the shaman and his assistant, in front of the temple.

ALSO UNDER THREAT

Other Mexican groups facing similar threats include the Seri, Yaqui, Raramuri (Tarahumara), Nahua, Triqui, Mixe, Zapoteco, Chol, Tzotzil, Tzeltal, Tojolabal and Lacandon.

Left Two Huichol men look across the mountain peaks and deep canyons of the Western Sierra Madre. It is one of the most remote, rugged areas of Mexico.

THE SACRED CACTUS

Every year the Huichol go on a pilgrimage to the desert of San Luis Potosi, 500 km away, to gather the peyote cactus. The cactus is sacred because it grows in the place where the first Huichol were said to have appeared, and by eating it today's Huichol have visions that connect them with the spirit world.

Peyote is used during important ceremonies, such as those held for the harvesting of crops and for deer hunts. Shamans also use peyote to help them diagnose illness.

SOUTH AMERICA

More than 19 million indigenous people live in South America today. Over 18 million of them are highland people like the Quechua and Aymara, while approximately one million live in lowland forest regions, including the Amazon and Orinoco river basins.

They are the descendants of people who moved down into the Americas about 30,000 years ago, gradually splitting into distinct peoples with their own languages and cultures and becoming experts in their own environments.

While some Amerindians have managed to cope with the threats for years (many Peruvian Quechua people now live in urban areas but have been able to keep much of their cultural identity), others are only now coming into contact with white people – usually with disastrous results. It is believed that there are still a few thousand uncontacted people in the lowland forests.

Amerindian cultures are still under threat today. Other South Americans will not allow Amerindians to keep their lands, or to control their own lives. The situation differs from country to country.

THE LAND, OUR MOTHER

'Ever since the white man first appeared, he has wanted to take our land and deprive us of our traditional and truthful laws...

'We must recover the land... because it is our mother, the source of our life and sustenance. We must recover our mother so that we can sustain our culture and our traditions and defend ourselves from the white man who is hemming us in more and more: herding us on to barren ground as if we were just pigs, fenced in to be fattened.'

Arhuaco elder, Colombia.

In Brazil, for example, Amerindians have no ownership rights over any land, while in Peru and Colombia, governments have recognized Amerindian ownership of large areas of territory.

However, across the continent lands are being dissected by roads, invaded by colonists and plundered for resources like minerals, timber and oil; rivers are being dammed and polluted. Indigenous languages and cultures are widely treated with contempt. Many peoples suffer brutal physical suppression by military regimes. White people's diseases such as 'flu, malaria, measles, tuberculosis and now AIDS are also major threats.

From the Andes mountains to the windswept islands of Tierra del Fuego, and from the Atacama desert to the tropical rain forests, the indigenous peoples represent a kaleidoscope of cultures, forming about 500 distinct groups.

Ever since Columbus landed in the Bahamas in 1492, the territories of the indigenous peoples of South America have been invaded and colonized, and culture after culture has been wiped out. Most Amerindian groups have lost up to ninety per cent of their populations within the first 10 years of contact with white people, largely through disease.

The threats facing South American indigenous peoples today are summarized and indicated by symbols in the key to the map opposite, which shows 101 threatened peoples.

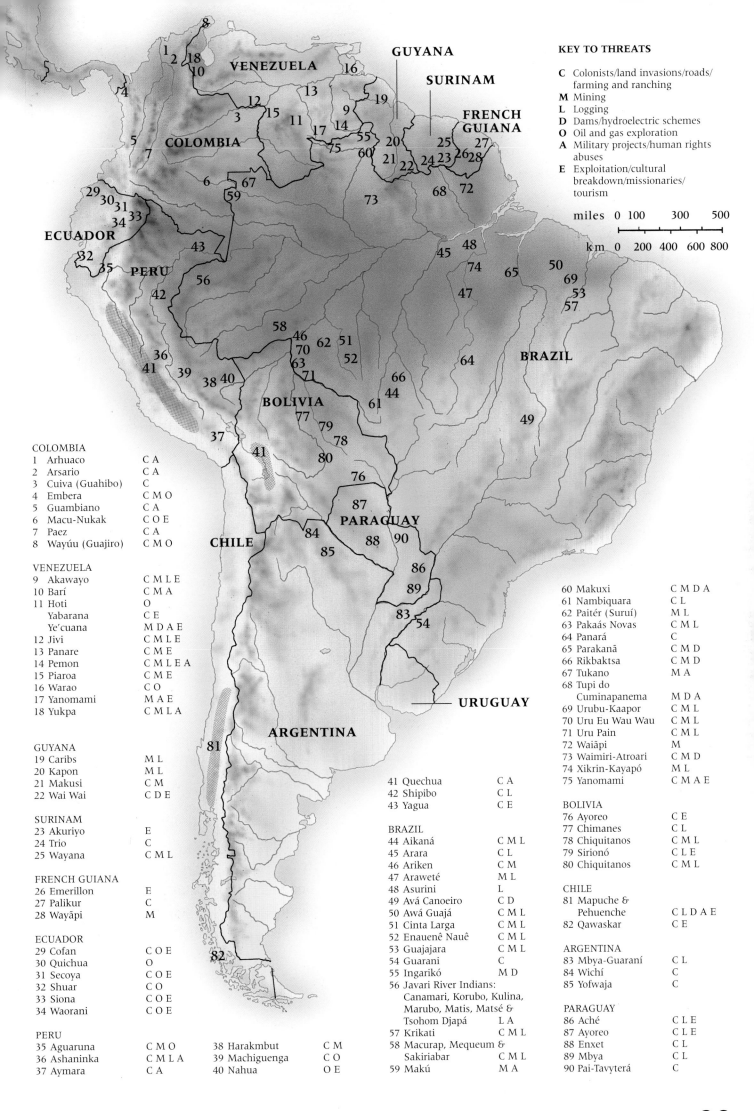

GUYANA
SURINAM
FRENCH
GUIANA
VENEZUELA
COLOMBIA
ECUADOR
PERU
BOLIVIA
CHILE
PARAGUAY
ARGENTINA
URUGUAY
BRAZIL

KEY TO THREATS

C Colonists/land invasions/roads/
farming and ranching
M Mining
L Logging
D Dams/hydroelectric schemes
O Oil and gas exploration
A Military projects/human rights
abuses
E Exploitation/cultural
breakdown/missionaries/
tourism

miles 0 100 300 500

km 0 200 400 600 800

COLOMBIA
1	Arhuaco	C A
2	Arsario	C A
3	Cuiva (Guahibo)	C
4	Embera	C M O
5	Guambiano	C A
6	Macu-Nukak	C O E
7	Paez	C A
8	Wayúu (Guajiro)	C M O

VENEZUELA
9	Akawayo	C M L E
10	Barí	C M A
11	Hoti	O
	Yabarana	C E
	Ye'cuana	M D A E
12	Jivi	C M L E
13	Panare	C M E
14	Pemon	C M L E A
15	Piaroa	C M E
16	Warao	C O
17	Yanomami	M A E
18	Yukpa	C M L A

GUYANA
19	Caribs	M L
20	Kapon	M L
21	Makusi	C M
22	Wai Wai	C D E

SURINAM
23	Akuriyo	E
24	Trio	C
25	Wayana	C M L

FRENCH GUIANA
26	Emerillon	E
27	Palikur	C
28	Wayãpi	M

ECUADOR
29	Cofan	C O E
30	Quichua	O
31	Secoya	C O E
32	Shuar	C O
33	Siona	C O E
34	Waorani	C O E

PERU
35	Aguaruna	C M O
36	Ashaninka	C M L A
37	Aymara	C A
38	Harakmbut	C M
39	Machiguenga	C O
40	Nahua	O E
41	Quechua	C A
42	Shipibo	C L
43	Yagua	C E

BRAZIL
44	Aikaná	C M L
45	Arara	C L
46	Ariken	C M
47	Araweté	M L
48	Asurini	L
49	Avá Canoeiro	C D
50	Awá Guajá	C M L
51	Cinta Larga	C M L
52	Enauenê Nauê	C M L
53	Guajajara	C M L
54	Guarani	C
55	Ingarikó	M D
56	Javari River Indians: Canamari, Korubo, Kulina, Marubo, Matis, Matsé & Tsohom Djapá	L A
57	Krikati	C M L
58	Macurap, Mequeum & Sakiriabar	C M L
59	Makú	M A
60	Makuxi	C M D A
61	Nambiquara	C L
62	Paitér (Suruí)	M L
63	Pakaás Novas	C M L
64	Panará	C
65	Parakanã	C M D
66	Rikbaktsa	C M D
67	Tukano	M A
68	Tupi do Cuminapanema	M D A
69	Urubu-Kaapor	C M L
70	Uru Eu Wau Wau	C M L
71	Uru Pain	C M L
72	Waiãpi	M
73	Waimiri-Atroari	C M D
74	Xikrin-Kayapó	M L
75	Yanomami	C M A E

BOLIVIA
76	Ayoreo	C E
77	Chimanes	C L
78	Chiquitanos	C M L
79	Sirionó	C L E
80	Chiquitanos	C M L

CHILE
81	Mapuche & Pehuenche	C L D A E
82	Qawaskar	C E

ARGENTINA
83	Mbya-Guaraní	C L
84	Wichí	C
85	Yofwaja	C

PARAGUAY
86	Aché	C L E
87	Ayoreo	C L E
88	Enxet	C L
89	Mbya	C L
90	Pai-Tavyterá	C

The Yanomami

The Yanomami are one of the largest groups of forest peoples in South America, still living traditionally in the Amazon rainforest. There are about 13,000 Yanomami in southern Venezuela and 8,000 in northern Brazil.

Whole villages, of between 25 and 400 people, live together in enormous communal houses – sometimes 40 metres across.

The Yanomami grow most of their food in forest gardens. The main crops are bananas and plantains, but sweet potatoes, cassava and maize are also important. About 60 crops are grown in all, including plants for medicines and religious rituals. Men hunt with bows and arrows, while fishing and farming are shared activities.

The first real threats to the Brazilian Yanomami began in the 1970s, when the *Perimetral Norte* (Northern Perimeter) road was cut through their lands. It allowed fatal diseases like 'flu, measles, malaria and tuberculosis to enter the region.

The Brazilian government refused to recognize the Yanomami's territory, and by 1989, 45,000 gold miners had invaded it, bringing diseases that killed about 1,500 people. Although the Yanomami Park was legally recognized in 1992, many gold miners still remain. They have destroyed countless river banks and streams, polluted the water and poisoned fish with mercury (now a serious problem in Amazonia). The Yanomami are also being murdered by the miners.

Made ill by a disease brought to her home by outsiders, a Yanomami woman is carried to an aeroplane that will take her to hospital.

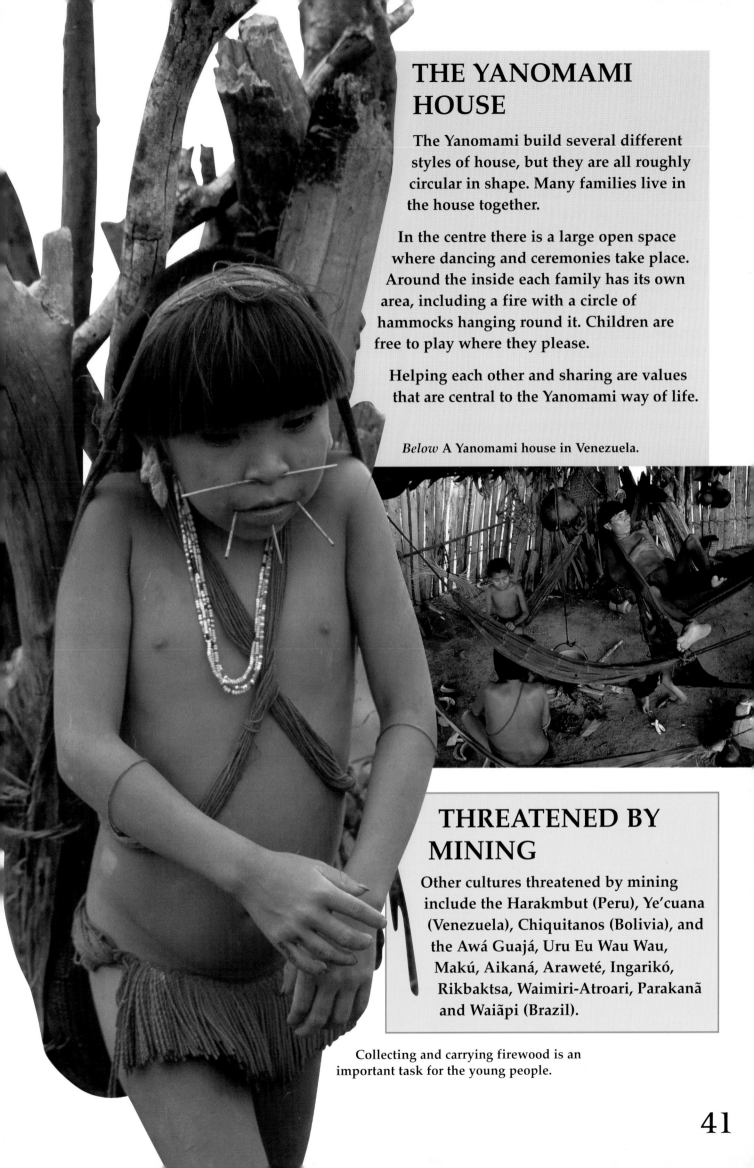

THE YANOMAMI HOUSE

The Yanomami build several different styles of house, but they are all roughly circular in shape. Many families live in the house together.

In the centre there is a large open space where dancing and ceremonies take place. Around the inside each family has its own area, including a fire with a circle of hammocks hanging round it. Children are free to play where they please.

Helping each other and sharing are values that are central to the Yanomami way of life.

Below A Yanomami house in Venezuela.

THREATENED BY MINING

Other cultures threatened by mining include the Harakmbut (Peru), Ye'cuana (Venezuela), Chiquitanos (Bolivia), and the Awá Guajá, Uru Eu Wau Wau, Makú, Aikaná, Araweté, Ingarikó, Rikbaktsa, Waimiri-Atroari, Parakanã and Waiãpi (Brazil).

Collecting and carrying firewood is an important task for the young people.

41

The Quechua

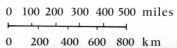

0 100 200 300 400 500 miles

0 200 400 600 800 km

The descendants of peoples once ruled by the great Inca empire, the Quechua are the largest indigenous nation in the Americas – about 14 million in all.

They live in the valleys, mountains and high plains of the Andes mountains – in Peru, where they form nearly half the population, and in Bolivia. Most Quechua today are poor farmers, living on small plots of land or working on haciendas.

In the warmer valleys many crops are grown, but in the high Andes people live largely by growing potatoes and herding animals (mostly llamas and sheep).

The Quechua's biggest problems concern the right to their land. Other people

PERU

BRAZIL

Lima

Nyachuco

Cuzco

BOLIVIA

PACIFIC
OCEAN

Lake Titicaca
La Paz

Cochamba

Oruro

Lake
Poopo

The Quechua

Today, most Quechua live in the Andes Mountains, although some have lost their land and had to leave. Their homes are mainly in Peru and Bolivia.

ALSO UNDER THREAT

Other peoples affected by the loss of their lands, military intervention and discrimination include the Mapuche and Pehuenche (Chile), Aymara (Peru and Bolivia), Arhuaco and Arsario (Colombia), Wayana (Surinam) the Javari River Indians, Makuxi and Tukano (Brazil), and the Barí, Pemon, Yanomami and Yukpa (Venezuela).

A young Quechua mother carries her baby on her back.

PACHA MAMA

These Quechua are threshing their crop of barley.

Most indigenous peoples believe that they belong to the land and must look after it. They believe that what they take from nature must be repaid in some way.

To the Quechua, *Pacha Mama* – the Earth Mother – protects all living things. She makes the crops grow and animals produce young. To repay her they must make offerings at certain times in the form of coca leaves and animal fat, and sprinkle *chicha* (maize beer) on the ground.

have taken more and more of their arable land, leaving smaller and smaller plots for their children. Many have been forced high into the mountains or off the land altogether, into cities where they can get only the worst, lowest-paid jobs.

Although Quechua is an official language in Peru, teachers often refuse to use it and children are made to feel ashamed of their origins. The Peruvian Quechua have suffered badly because of the guerrilla organization 'The Shining Path'. They have been caught in the crossfire between the terrorists and the army, and many have been killed.

This woman, dressed in a brightly coloured traditional outfit, has come to market in Pisac, Peru, to sell her bread.

43

The Wichí

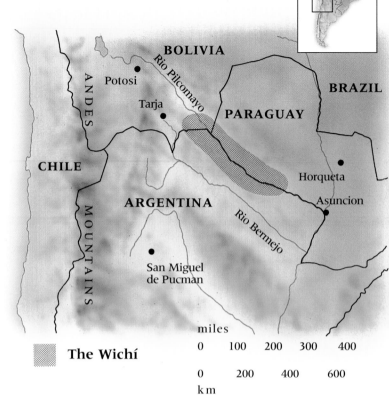

The Wichí live in north-eastern Argentina, south-eastern Bolivia and western Paraguay, in the semi-arid region of scrubby forest known as the Chaco. Throughout the year they hunt animals including deer, armadillos, peccaries and iguanas, and collect wild fruit and nuts, as well as honey. During the winter months the Wichí depend largely on fish for food. In the summer they grow maize, beans, watermelons and pumpkins in their gardens.

Numbering up to 40,000 people all together, about 20,000 Wichí live in north-eastern Argentina. Here, the Wichí's problems started at the beginning of the twentieth century when the first settlers arrived and began to take over their lands for houses and farms.

This man is smoking bees from their hive. The honey he will collect is a tasty treat for the Wichí.

44

A group of Wichí in front of their field of maize.

The settlers began to harass the Wichí and hunt them down. This process continues today. Well-armed settlers have introduced herds of cattle that have turned much fertile land into sandy desert.

This old Wichí woman has seen years of change for her people, as they have slowly been forced off their lands.

FISHING

The Pilcomayo River flows through the territory of the Wichí and they are expert fishermen.

They catch over eighteen different kinds of fish including a catfish (*afwukna*), a kind of salmon (*atsa*) and white shad (*sichus*). When the river is low – in winter – the Wichí wade waist-deep into the muddy water. Able to detect the fish by movements on the water's surface, they plunge a net strung between two poles into the water and pull up their catch.

In 1987 a law was passed giving settlers legal rights to Wichí land. In 1991 the Wichí made a map of their area and carried out a survey to show what belonged to them. Soon after, a decree was passed recognizing the Wichí's ownership of their land, but in 1995 they still had not received their communal land titles.

ALSO UNDER THREAT

Hundreds of other cultures are threatened by colonists and ranchers. They include the Avá Canoeiro, Guarani and Panará in Brazil, the Akawayo and Warao in Venezuela, and the

EUROPE AND THE MIDDLE EAST

Europe and the Middle East are the territory of old and well-established civilizations, and in many ways the battle between threatened cultures and encroaching strangers no longer exists in the same way as it does, for example, in South America. Often, the battle has been long since won by the majority.

Nevertheless there are still many cases where small groups of people, like the Gypsies of Eastern and Western Europe, are in danger of ceasing to exist as identifiable communities, and other cases, like that of the Kurds in the Middle East, where a large population, with its own distinct language and culture, is in danger because of clashes with governments in the region.

A number of the threatened cultures of the Middle East and Europe are nomadic, and the

A Bedouin man with his flock of sheep in Syria.

threat to them arises in part from the intolerance of settled cultures to nomads. Another threat comes from economics: in the modern world, it is harder to make a living from traditional nomadic pursuits.

These Gypsies in Porumbacu, Romania, are mending buckets and other household items to earn money.

KEY TO THREATS
A Threat to religion
B Sedentarization of nomads
C Economic threat to livelihood
D Assimilation to majority culture
E Threat to minority language
F Pressure to emigrate

EUROPE

Ireland

13 Gypsies	B C D

UK

13 Gypsies	B C D
21 Scots Gaelic Speakers	E

France

13 Gypsies	B C D
15 Bretons	E
21 Basques	E

Spain

13 Gypsies	B C D

Germany

13 Gypsies	B C D
19 East European Jews	A D

Italy

16 French speakers	E
17 German speakers	E

Greece

18 Pomak Muslims	A D

Austria

13 Gypsies	B C D
19 East European Jews	A D

Bulgaria

13 Gypsies	B C D

Romania

13 Gypsies	B C D

Slovakia

13 Gypsies	B C D
19 East European Jews	A D

Czech Republic

13 Gypsies	B C D
19 East European Jews	A D

Poland

13 Gypsies	B C D
19 East European Jews	A D

Ukraine

13 Gypsies	B C D
19 East European Jews	A D

Russia

13 Gypsies	B C D
19 East European Jews	A D

Belarus

13 Gypsies	B C D
19 East European Jews	A D

Estonia/Latvia/Lithuania

20 Russian Minority	F

EUROPE AND
THE MIDDLE EAST (cont.)

Another threat to cultures is linguistic. Some people are in danger of losing an old minority tongue to the spread of a majority language, which is usually spoken by the government and the media and so is more powerful. Such communities are usually in no physical danger but stand to lose their cultural heritage and have their identity changed.

Finally the Jews of Eastern Europe, who have a profound and ancient culture, are in danger of losing their distinctiveness. In many countries, their population numbers are dropping as a result of emigration, and very often the more isolated individual members of the remaining group are merging with the mainstream societies.

HOPE AND FEAR

'For as long as I can remember, I have tried to understand the nature of Kurdistan and the Kurds. During my childhood I had to watch while tanks crushed the houses of our neighbours, and see how time and again schoolfriends of mine would disappear, not to be seen again, or how the parents of Kurdish guerrilla fighters were taken away by the Iraqi secret service. I learned that the struggle for the freedom of the Kurds was a struggle in which lives were at risk. But I also learned to understand the joy and the will to live of my people. Hope and fear seem to me to be so inseparably linked together in no other nation.'

Namo Aziz, *Kurdistan*, (DA Verlag Das Andere, 1992; translated from the German by John King)

Nomadic Kurds have set up this camp in eastern Turkey. About a quarter of Kurds in Turkey belong to a minority Muslim group called the Alevis.

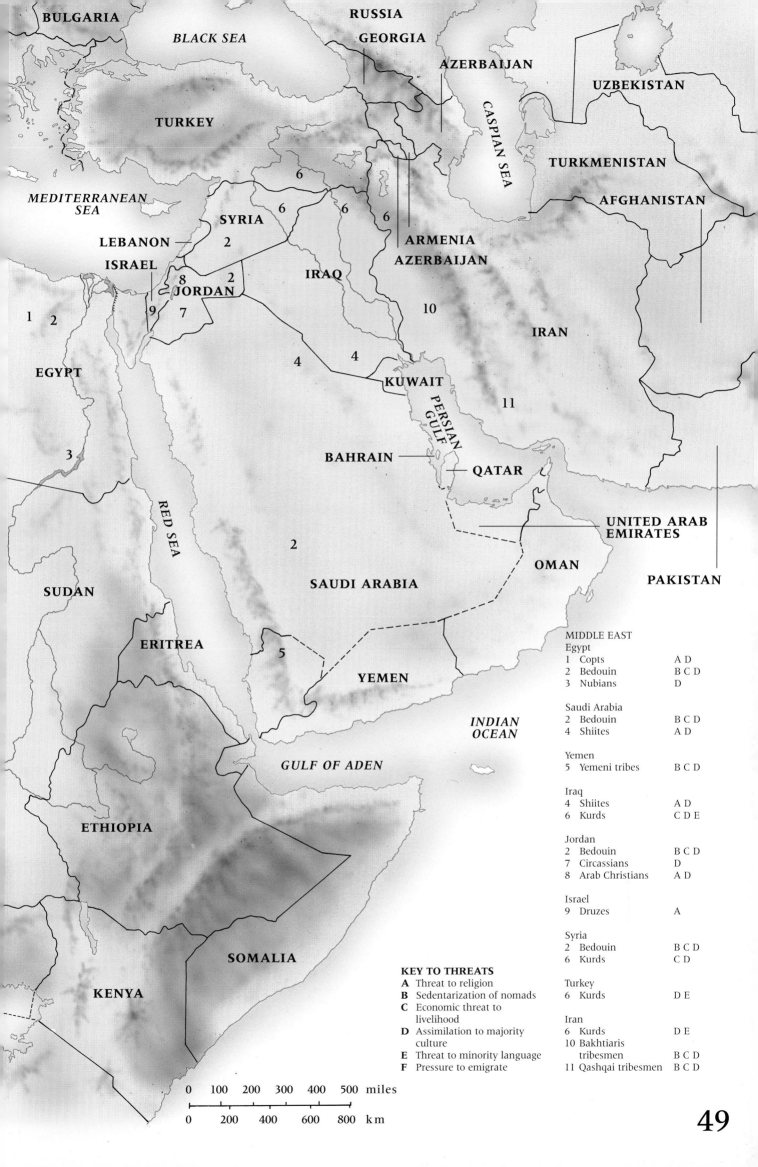

BULGARIA

BLACK SEA

RUSSIA

GEORGIA

AZERBAIJAN

UZBEKISTAN

CASPIAN SEA

TURKEY

TURKMENISTAN

MEDITERRANEAN SEA

6

6

6

6

SYRIA

2

ARMENIA

AZERBAIJAN

AFGHANISTAN

LEBANON

ISRAEL

8

2

IRAQ

JORDAN

9

7

10

IRAN

1   2

EGYPT

4   4

KUWAIT

11

PERSIAN GULF

3

BAHRAIN

QATAR

RED SEA

2

UNITED ARAB EMIRATES

OMAN

PAKISTAN

SUDAN

SAUDI ARABIA

ERITREA

5

YEMEN

INDIAN OCEAN

ETHIOPIA

GULF OF ADEN

SOMALIA

KENYA

MIDDLE EAST
Egypt

1	Copts	A D
2	Bedouin	B C D
3	Nubians	D

Saudi Arabia

| 2 | Bedouin | B C D |
| 4 | Shiites | A D |

Yemen

| 5 | Yemeni tribes | B C D |

Iraq

| 4 | Shiites | A D |
| 6 | Kurds | C D E |

Jordan

2	Bedouin	B C D
7	Circassians	D
8	Arab Christians	A D

Israel

| 9 | Druzes | A |

Syria

| 2 | Bedouin | B C D |
| 6 | Kurds | C D |

KEY TO THREATS

A Threat to religion
B Sedentarization of nomads
C Economic threat to livelihood
D Assimilation to majority culture
E Threat to minority language
F Pressure to emigrate

Turkey

| 6 | Kurds | D E |

Iran

6	Kurds	D E
10	Bakhtiaris tribesmen	B C D
11	Qashqai tribesmen	B C D

0   100   200   300   400   500   miles

0   200   400   600   800   km

49

The Kurds

The Kurds have struggled hard during the twentieth century to have a country of their own, which they would call Kurdistan. They hoped that after the end of the First World War the League of Nations would recognize their national identity and give them a place of their own, but their land was divided between other countries.

The 22 million Kurds now live mostly in Turkey, Iraq, Syria and Iran, and this division among four countries is the heart of their problem. The Kurds see themselves as a whole nation, and they believe they are denied their right to a separate existence by the Middle East countries they inhabit.

The Kurds have been subjected to terrible persecution, especially in Iraq, where many thousands died and lost their homes during

A Kurdish family on the move in Kurdistan, Iran.

the long war between Iraq and Iran from 1980 to 1988. Persecution continued after the Gulf War (1991), when large numbers of Kurds fled to the autonomous enclave in which they now live in northern Iraq. There is also a Kurdish separatist movement in Turkey, which is harshly repressed by the security forces.

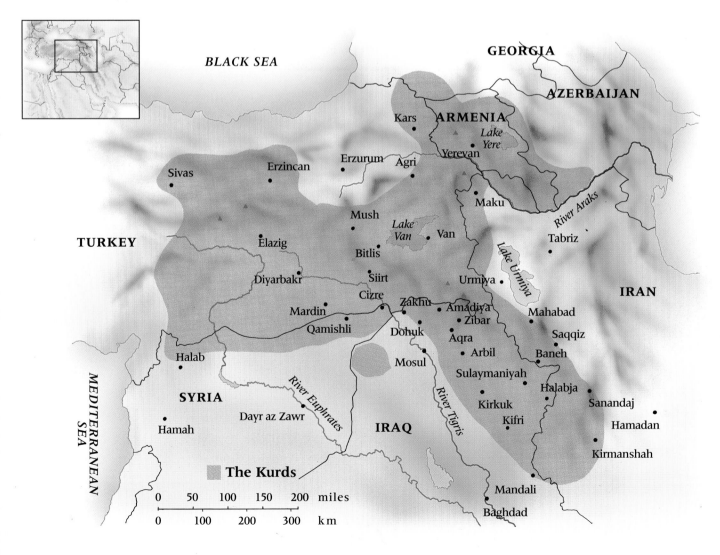

The way of life of the Kurds is based on farming and keeping flocks and herds, though of course in the towns the Kurds are also their own shopkeepers, schoolteachers, local government officials and doctors. They have their own language, and there are traditional Kurdish clothes which are still worn in the countryside. The men wear baggy trousers and a Western jacket, with a turban headdress tied in a traditional way. The women's clothes are brightly coloured and often embroidered. As they are farming and herding people, their staple food is bread, and meat is eaten on special occasions.

THE KURDISH LANGUAGE

The countries in which the Kurds live have not encouraged the use of the Kurdish language. In Turkey Kurdish was absolutely forbidden until recently, and its use is still restricted. The Kurds have always had to accept that their children will be educated in the majority language of the country where they live: Turkish in Turkey, Arabic in Iraq and Syria, and Farsi in Iran. The Kurdish language is written down in different ways: in Arabic script in Iraq, and European script in Turkey.

The Kurds are Muslims, belonging mostly to mainstream Sunni Islam. There are some Shiite Kurds in Iran, and another small Muslim sect, the Yezidis. About a quarter of Turkey's Kurds belong to a minority Muslim group called the Alevis.

The Kurds have their own music and folksongs. Some of these songs are regarded as the anthems of the Kurdish nationalist movement. Many Kurds have emigrated to Europe, where the largest numbers live in Germany, and concerts of Kurdish music in Germany's big cities attract huge audiences.

Kurdish refugees on the Turkish border in Iraq. Kurds in Iraq have been badly persecuted and have suffered terribly. Many now live in awful conditions in refugee camps like this one.

European Gypsies

The Gypsies came originally from India, but they have been in Europe for more than 600 years. They are a nomadic people, who get their living from trading with the people of the countries they inhabit. Gypsies usually prefer not to take jobs, other than temporary work, and the Gypsies in Western Europe often prefer to live in caravans rather than in houses.

and there are traditional Gypsy trades, such as charcoal burning. East European Gypsies are also entertainers, dancing and playing musical instruments like the accordion and the violin.

Gypsy culture is more distinct in Eastern Europe than in the West, but all Gypsies are aware of their traditions and customs and of the Gypsy language, in which they take much pride. In Eastern Europe, Gypsies wear distinctive clothes. The women cover their hair and wear embroidered skirts and other colourful garments.

Gypsies make a distinction between themselves and non-Gypsies, who are known as *gaje*. They also have customs that set them apart from other travellers. For example, they have a very strict rule about keeping water and utensils used for cooking separate from those used for washing and personal hygiene.

Gypsies dancing at the International Festival of Gypsies in the Czech Republic.

In the West, Gypsies do a variety of work, such as farm labour, building work, and buying and selling cars. Their traditional occupation is horse trading, but they now mainly sell horses to each other, so this is not an occupation that brings money into the community. Gypsy women traditionally make and sell objects such as clothes pegs, and do fortune-telling.

In Eastern Europe, the Gypsies are more settled. They have settlements and villages,

British gypsies with their brightly coloured caravans. Traditionally, gypsy caravans are horse drawn.

These Roma and Sinti Gypsies are holding a street occupation in Hamburg, Germany, to demonstrate against deportation.

THE CARAVAN

Gypsy caravans are always neat inside and sometimes give the appearance of luxury. Gypsies who can afford the expense aspire to have a gleaming motor-drawn trailer with a TV and a stereo system. Gypsy caravans often seem to be surrounded by discarded objects: many of these will be scrap awaiting sorting for sale. A fire may be kept burning to dispose of rubbish. Even after several months at a site, a Gypsy family can be ready to move in an hour or two if necessary.

Eating together is regarded as a sign of friendship by Gypsies. There are various ways in which a person can become 'unclean'. Some Gypsies have their own justice system, called the *kris*, and religious beliefs of their own, though others have become Christians.

Gypsies are threatened by assimilation into the mainstream culture, and by governments' desire to settle them. Many people mistrust Gypsies and think they are dishonest. However, they survived in the past because the particular kinds of work they did were valuable to society. Today in Western Europe, work is hard to find and it is difficult for travelling Gypsies to find places to stay. There is sharp hostility to Gypsy refugees in Germany. But anti-Gypsy feeling is strongest in Eastern Europe, where Gypsies have been killed in attacks on their villages in Romania.

The map shows the countries in Europe which have large numbers of Gypsies, or where Gypsies form a significant proportion of the population.

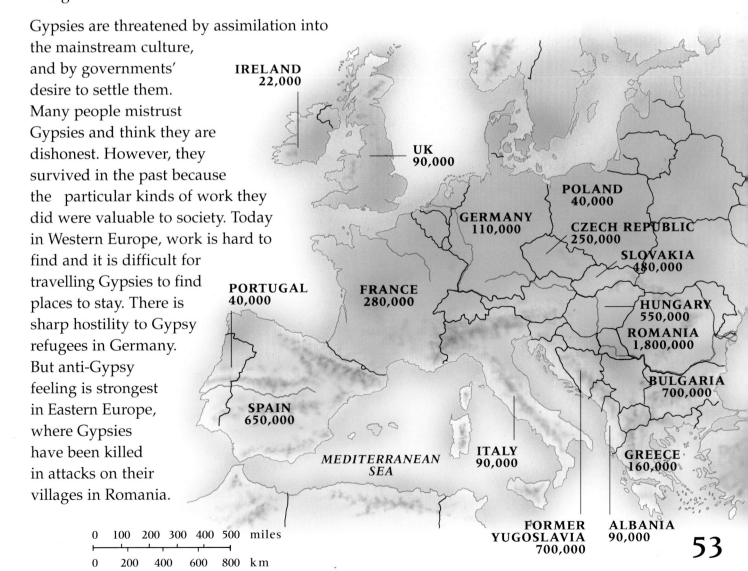

IRELAND
22,000

UK
90,000

POLAND
40,000

GERMANY
110,000

CZECH REPUBLIC
250,000

SLOVAKIA
480,000

PORTUGAL
40,000

FRANCE
280,000

HUNGARY
550,000

ROMANIA
1,800,000

BULGARIA
700,000

SPAIN
650,000

MEDITERRANEAN
SEA

ITALY
90,000

GREECE
160,000

| 0 | 100 | 200 | 300 | 400 | 500 | miles |

| 0 | 200 | 400 | 600 | 800 | km |

FORMER
YUGOSLAVIA
700,000

ALBANIA
90,000

53

The Bedouin

A housing estate at Al Ain, Abu Dhabi, built to house Bedouin. Most Bedouin refuse to live there and so the estate is left deserted and soulless.

The Bedouin live in harsh surroundings, making a living from the land, their flocks and handicrafts in an environment that settled people would regard as impossible to live in. The Bedouin heartland is the great desert that lies across the interior of Saudi Arabia, Jordan and Syria. There are also Bedouin in Egypt and in North African countries, including Tunisia and Libya.

The Bedouin live by keeping flocks and herds. Traditionally, the Bedouin kept camels, but in less harsh areas on the edge of the desert they also have flocks of sheep. The Bedouin are traders, buying and selling dates and other goods. They also sell handicrafts and do agricultural work on farms in oasis settlements and on the desert rim. Traditionally they live in clusters of tents, and move from one place to another in search of better pastures, fresh water or better weather.

The independent way of life of the Bedouin is seen as a threat by many Arab governments, who would prefer them to live in settled villages. Some governments, including Egypt's, offer the Bedouin free housing if they will settle down in one place. But another threat to their existence is the difficulty of making enough money to live on without taking jobs for regular wages.

A Bedouin warrior on horseback in the Sahara Desert, Tunisia.

A Bedouin family on the move to a new camp, crossing the desert by camel.

The attitude of Arab people towards the Bedouin is ambiguous. On the one hand, they believe that Arab culture came from the desert and that the Bedouin are the guardians of an important cultural heritage, embodying the Arab ideals of independence, dignity and hospitality. On the other hand, settled people may distrust and look down on the Bedouin because of their poverty and the belief that Bedouin may steal and are untrustworthy.

THE CAMEL

Traditional Bedouin economy depended on the camel. This animal can travel great distances across the desert without water and in the past was vital to the Bedouin way of life. The camels provided milk, and wool for weaving cloth, carpets and tents. They could also be slaughtered to produce meat to eat. The ownership of camels was a symbol of wealth, and Bedouin men set great store by their ability to drive a good bargain in buying and selling camels. Today, though, a tough four-wheel drive vehicle may be preferred by many Bedouin.

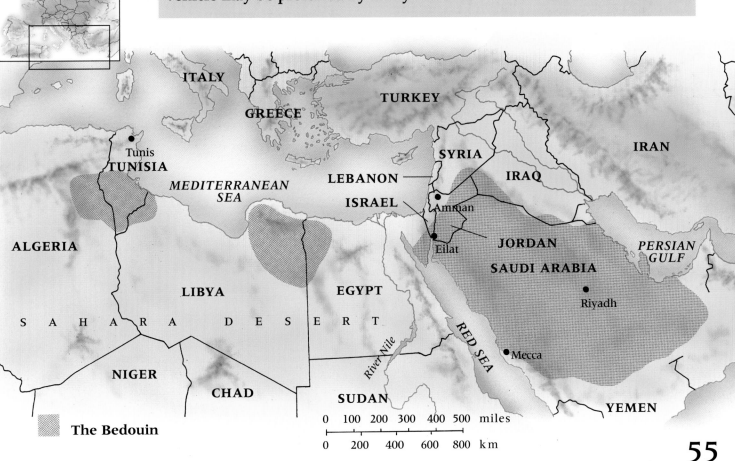

The Bedouin

Russian and Ukrainian Jews

The Jewish presence in Russia and the former Soviet countries dates back 400 years, and a distinctively Russian Jewish culture grew up there. During the nineteenth century, Jews in Russia often lived in Jewish villages. They were traders; later many became professionals such as lawyers and doctors. A village where Jews lived was known as a *shtetl*.

The Ashkenazi Jews, as the Jews of Germany and Eastern Europe are known, had their own language, Yiddish, and a strong literary tradition. Yiddish is a version of German, with the addition of Hebrew and other words, and was carried across Europe by the Jews from their earlier homes in Germany, Poland and Lithuania. However, Ashkenazi Jews today mainly speak Russian.

There has also been a strong tradition of Jewish cookery and Jewish folk music in Eastern Europe. Traditional Jewish dishes that came from Eastern Europe include salt beef, gefilte fish, potato pancakes known as *latkes*, and chicken soup with noodles. Jewish music is characterized by a virtuoso style of violin playing and by music for wind instruments – particularly the clarinet – which is known as *klezmer* music.

Jews put a high value on intellectual activity, and the Russian Jewish community has produced brilliant musicians, mathematicians and chess players. But from the Russian pogroms of the nineteenth century up to the organized anti-Semitism of Hitler's Germany, the Jews have faced persecution. Even in Russia today, they face anti-Semitism, which denies them jobs and career advancement.

By 1993 a million Jews had left Russia and Ukraine. Most went to Israel, but many are now choosing to go to the United States or elsewhere in the West. Today demographers estimate there are less than half a million Jews in the former territory of the Soviet Union. The remaining Jews in Russia and Ukraine are becoming highly assimilated and soon they will be hard to distinguish from other Russians and Ukrainians.

Rabbis praying in a synagogue in Moscow, Russia.

Map

0 100 200 300 400 miles

0 200 400 600 km

Russian and Ukrainian Jews

LITHUANIA

ESTONIA

St Petersburg

LATVIA

River Volga

Moscow

Minsk

BELARUS

RUSSIA

UKRAINE

Kiev

River Don

River Dnieper

Odessa

ROMANIA

MOLDAVIA

BLACK SEA

KOSHER FOOD

A key element of Jewish culture is kosher food. Jews have strict dietary laws which control what they are permitted to eat and how they prepare food. There are also complicated rules that govern the slaughter of animals to be eaten. Jews are not allowed to eat pork, and in a strictly orthodox Jewish kitchen separate sets of plates are kept for meat and milk products, which may not be eaten at the same meal. With the assimilation and dispersion of the Jewish community in Russia, it becomes harder to stick to these rules, which contributes to the dilution of the Jews' sense of their separate identity.

A sabbath brunch for elderly men at a synagogue in Kiev, Russia. The man in black is wearing the traditional clothes of a strict Orthodox Jew.

AFRICA

Africa is sometimes called 'the cradle of humankind'. All the peoples of the earth are descended from Africans who migrated northwards and eastwards, to the other continents, about 50,000 years ago. Today the population of Africa is over 750 million.

Geographically, Africa is a varied continent. Some areas are extremely dry, and other areas have high rainfall, rivers and lakes. In the north and the south there are great deserts (the Sahara and the Kalahari). Much of the rest of Africa is covered with grassland or savannah, and some is mountainous. Only in Central Africa is there deep forest or jungle.

The peoples of Africa are also varied. Some live in harsh, dry areas where it is very difficult to grow food. Most Africans are farmers, but even good farming regions have been affected by drought. Lack of water affects many parts of Africa, from Somalia in the east to Mauritania in the west. It is a major cause of famine. Another cause of famine is illness. Malaria, tuberculosis and AIDS are common. Even if people survive serious illness, they may be unable to sow or harvest crops while they are ill.

At one time Arab traders and European colonists controlled most of Africa. In recent times, powerful groups within Africa – such as the former regimes in Ethiopia and Malawi – have oppressed small minorities, stealing their land and imprisoning or killing them. In the past, people were forced into slavery; now they are made to work for feudal masters or have to migrate to find jobs. There are wars in several parts of the continent. Some have been going on for years.

Some peoples face the threat of cultural assimilation by a neighbouring group. This means that they are forced, either by other groups or just by circumstances, to change their religion, their language or the way they dress to fit in with others. It can mean that peoples will lose their culture entirely, and their pride too. Groups that lose their culture often become assimilated at the bottom level of society. This means they get less land and have lower status than their neighbours.

The threats facing African peoples are summarized in the key to the map opposite. Some groups, such as Bushmen, Pygmies and Tuareg, can be divided into several different peoples, each with their own slightly different language or culture and their own identity.

A Maasai tribesman with a headdress of ostrich feathers.

THE SPIRITS OF THE FOREST

'When things aren't going well we sing, crying to the forest, to our ancestors: "Don't turn your backs on us". The forest and the ancestors are the same, they are one. When we sing to them to ask their blessings that the forest be full of meat, we call on the grandparents of our grandparents. It is the forest, the ancestors, who give to us the things we need.'

Amozati Kanjalai, a Mbuti elder from Zaire

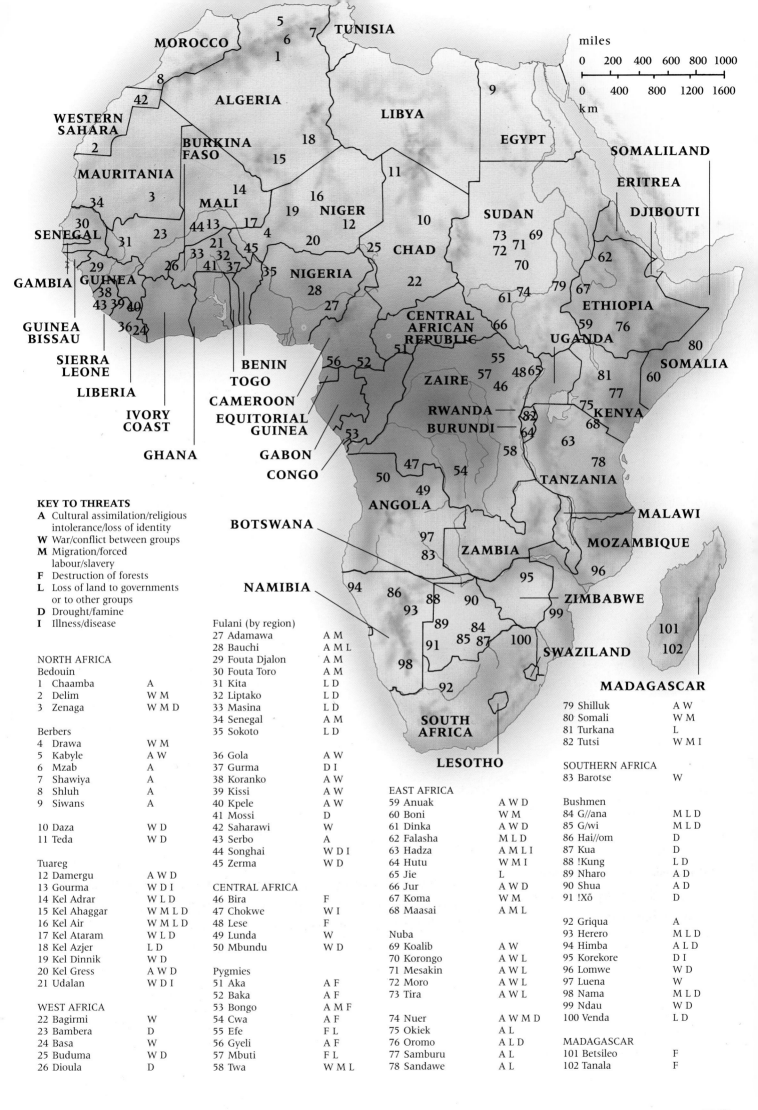

Map of African ethnic groups and threats. Country labels include: MOROCCO, TUNISIA, ALGERIA, LIBYA, EGYPT, WESTERN SAHARA, MAURITANIA, MALI, NIGER, CHAD, SUDAN, ERITREA, SOMALILAND, DJIBOUTI, BURKINA FASO, SENEGAL, GAMBIA, GUINEA, GUINEA BISSAU, SIERRA LEONE, LIBERIA, IVORY COAST, GHANA, BENIN, TOGO, NIGERIA, CAMEROON, EQUITORIAL GUINEA, GABON, CONGO, CENTRAL AFRICAN REPUBLIC, ETHIOPIA, SOMALIA, UGANDA, ZAIRE, RWANDA, BURUNDI, KENYA, TANZANIA, ANGOLA, BOTSWANA, NAMIBIA, ZAMBIA, MALAWI, MOZAMBIQUE, ZIMBABWE, SOUTH AFRICA, LESOTHO, SWAZILAND, MADAGASCAR.

KEY TO THREATS

A Cultural assimilation/religious intolerance/loss of identity
W War/conflict between groups
M Migration/forced labour/slavery
F Destruction of forests
L Loss of land to governments or to other groups
D Drought/famine
I Illness/disease

NORTH AFRICA

Bedouin
1	Chaamba	A
2	Delim	W M
3	Zenaga	W M D

Berbers
4	Drawa	W M
5	Kabyle	A W
6	Mzab	A
7	Shawiya	A
8	Shluh	A
9	Siwans	A

10	Daza	W D
11	Teda	W D

Tuareg
12	Damergu	A W D
13	Gourma	W D I
14	Kel Adrar	W L D
15	Kel Ahaggar	W M L D
16	Kel Air	W M L D
17	Kel Ataram	W L D
18	Kel Azjer	L D
19	Kel Dinnik	W D
20	Kel Gress	A W D
21	Udalan	W D I

WEST AFRICA
22	Bagirmi	W
23	Bambera	D
24	Basa	W
25	Buduma	W D
26	Dioula	D

Fulani (by region)
27	Adamawa	A M
28	Bauchi	A M L
29	Fouta Djalon	A M
30	Fouta Toro	A M
31	Kita	L D
32	Liptako	L D
33	Masina	L D
34	Senegal	A M
35	Sokoto	L D

36	Gola	A W
37	Gurma	D I
38	Koranko	A W
39	Kissi	A W
40	Kpele	A W
41	Mossi	D
42	Saharawi	W
43	Serbo	A
44	Songhai	W D I
45	Zerma	W D

CENTRAL AFRICA
46	Bira	F
47	Chokwe	W I
48	Lese	F
49	Lunda	W
50	Mbundu	W D

Pygmies
51	Aka	A F
52	Baka	A F
53	Bongo	A M F
54	Cwa	A F
55	Efe	F L
56	Gyeli	A F
57	Mbuti	F L
58	Twa	W M L

EAST AFRICA
59	Anuak	A W D
60	Boni	W M
61	Dinka	A W D
62	Falasha	M L D
63	Hadza	A M L I
64	Hutu	W M I
65	Jie	L
66	Jur	A W D
67	Koma	W M
68	Maasai	A M L

Nuba
69	Koalib	A W
70	Korongo	A W L
71	Mesakin	A W L
72	Moro	A W L
73	Tira	A W L

74	Nuer	A W M D
75	Okiek	A L
76	Oromo	A L D
77	Samburu	A L
78	Sandawe	A L
79	Shilluk	A W
80	Somali	W M
81	Turkana	L
82	Tutsi	W M I

SOUTHERN AFRICA
83	Barotse	W

Bushmen
84	G//ana	M L D
85	G/wi	M L D
86	Hai//om	D
87	Kua	D
88	!Kung	L D
89	Nharo	A D
90	Shua	A D
91	!Xõ	D

92	Griqua	A
93	Herero	M L D
94	Himba	A L D
95	Korekore	D I
96	Lomwe	W D
97	Luena	W
98	Nama	M L D
99	Ndau	W D
100	Venda	L D

MADAGASCAR
101	Betsileo	F
102	Tanala	F

The !Kung

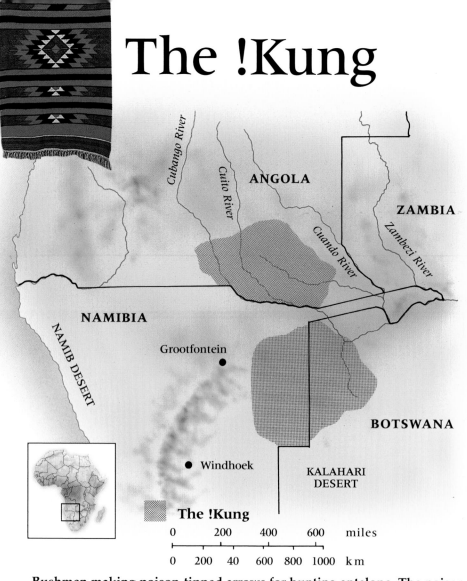

The !Kung are the largest group of the people known as Bushmen or San. There are probably about 30,000 to 35,000 !Kung, mainly in Botswana and Namibia. They traditionally lived by hunting and gathering over wide areas of land.

In recent years there have been severe threats from neighbouring groups such as the Herero who have taken their lands, from government schemes and from natural disasters, mainly drought.

In Botswana, drought has affected !Kung for most of the last twenty years. !Kung used to have many water holes and

Bushmen making poison-tipped arrows for hunting antelope. The poison comes from beetle larvae.

a large variety of wild plants, as well as great numbers of wild animals to hunt. These plants and animals depend on water, so without water the !Kung have little to eat.

Drought has also affected the !Kung of Namibia. In both countries, !Kung have to share their water holes with cattle herders, whose animals drink large amounts of water and eat the grass on which wild animals depend. During the Namibian civil war, which ended in 1989, soldiers moved !Kung from their land, so many !Kung children have not been able to learn the traditional hunting and gathering techniques.

There are also !Kung in Angola. A civil war there has destroyed their livelihood and forced many to flee from their lands. Some Angolan !Kung have gone to Namibia to try to start a new life, but they have had trouble finding land and being accepted.

SOUNDS OF THE !KUNG LANGUAGE

!Kung is an unusual language with strange 'click' sounds. There are four special symbols to show these sounds in writing.

/   A sucking sound, like the English expression of annoyance, 'tsk tsk'.

≠   A sharp movement of the tongue. It sounds like a harsh hand clap.

//   A different 'click' sound, much like the one cowboys use to make their horses go.

!   This sounds like a cork coming out of a bottle. It is made by popping the tongue away from the roof of the mouth.

ALSO UNDER THREAT

Other southern African cultures threatened by drought include the Nama and Hai//om (Namibia), G/wi, G//ana and Kua (Botswana), Korekore (Zimbabwe) and Venda (South Africa).

Above Cattle on the edge of the Kalahari Desert. The scrubland is being eroded as the desert spreads further on to it.

Right A medicine man from a Bushman band. He has an important role within the band, curing people using herbal remedies.

The Mbuti

The Mbuti are one of several groups of Pygmies, small people – rarely taller than 1.5 m – who live in Central Africa. No one knows how many Mbuti there are, but the total Pygmy population is less than 100,000.

The Mbuti live deep in the Ituri rainforest of Zaire. Like the !Kung, they have traditionally hunted and gathered wild foods for their livelihood. Over the past 40 years road builders, mining companies, coffee and cotton planters, and even warring armies have all moved into Mbuti country. These activities have caused much trouble for the Mbuti and the other people who live in and around the forest. The danger to the Mbuti way of life is now greater than ever.

The main danger today is from forestry. International logging companies have bought the rights to cut down large areas of the forest and sell the high-grade wood abroad. This destroys not only the forest itself, but the plants and animals on which the Mbuti and their neighbours depend.

ALSO UNDER THREAT

Other Pygmy cultures threatened by destruction of the forests of Central Africa include the Efe (Zaire), Aka (Congo and Central African Republic), Baka and Gyeli (Cameroon) and Twa (Zaire, Rwanda and Burundi).

Left **A Pygmy wearing a fur headdress.**

Above **Large areas of the Ituri forest have been cut down for timber.**

SUDAN

ZAIRE

Ituri River

Lindi River

Zaire River Kisangami

UGANDA

Equator

Lualaba River

RWANDA

Lake Victoria

BURUNDI

TANZANIA

The Mbuti

0   100   200   miles

0   100   200   300   400   km

FOREST AND VILLAGE

The Mbuti spend part of the year living deep in the Ituri forest in groups of between 15 and 40 people. They spend the rest of the year on the edges of the villages of neighbouring farming peoples such as the Bira.

The Mbuti and Bira trade with each other and share in the same sacred rituals, called *molimos*, which help them to remember the forest spirits of their forefathers.

Mbuti Pygmies in their village in the Ituri forest. A discarded truck tyre makes a functional seat in the centre of the village.

The Maasai

Girls dancing at one of the many Maasai tribal ceremonies.

The Maasai cattle herders are among the most famous of all African peoples. Yet they number less than one per cent of the population of Kenya and Tanzania, and their customs are under threat.

In some parts of Kenya, unscrupulous officials have taken Maasai land. This has been going on since the 1970s, even at the foot of the sacred Ngong Hills near Nairobi. The people who have taken the land do not even want it to grow things for themselves, but to make money from it. Some are now selling the land, which they have no legal right to do. Maasai who have protested have been sent to prison, while the local officials are getting rich.

In 1980 the Kenyan government banned all organizations that were recruited on an ethnic basis. Many Kenyans thought this was a good thing, because it meant that all people would be considered equal. But it has not stopped the

MAASAI AGE GRADES

Maasai pass through several stages called age grades. Each grade has specific activities. Maasai girls fetch water and firewood and milk the cows and goats. Boys spend their time learning how to look after the livestock.

At about 16, both girls and boys are initiated into adulthood. A young woman may then marry an older man, while a young man becomes a *murran* (warrior). For the next 10 or 12 years he lives in a special camp with others initiated at the same time. In his late twenties he will be initiated again, this time as an elder. Male elders can marry and take part in making decisions for the people.

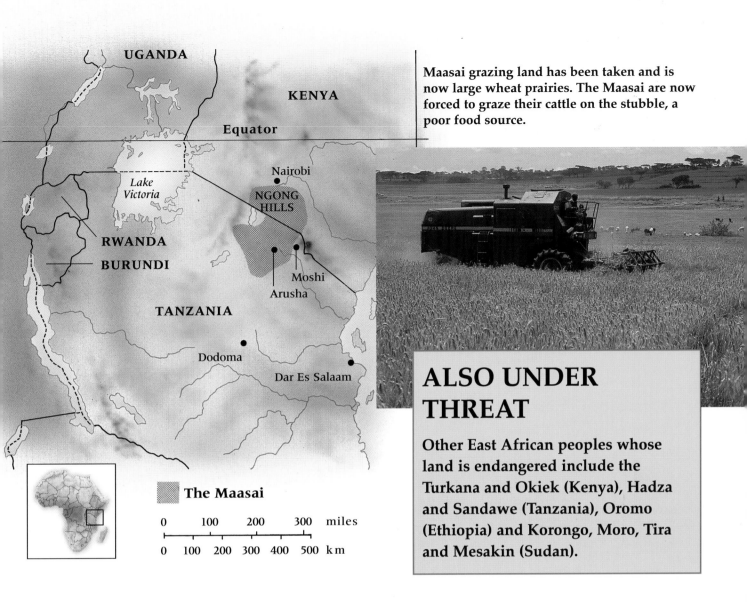

Maasai grazing land has been taken and is now large wheat prairies. The Maasai are now forced to graze their cattle on the stubble, a poor food source.

NGONG HILLS

UGANDA

KENYA

Equator

Nairobi

Lake Victoria

RWANDA

BURUNDI

Moshi

Arusha

TANZANIA

Dodoma

Dar Es Salaam

The Maasai

0   100   200   300   miles

0   100   200 300   400   500 km

ALSO UNDER THREAT

Other East African peoples whose land is endangered include the Turkana and Okiek (Kenya), Hadza and Sandawe (Tanzania), Oromo (Ethiopia) and Korongo, Moro, Tira and Mesakin (Sudan).

larger and richer groups, such as the Kikuyu, from dominating. For example, some districts get more government funding than others, and small minorities like the Maasai find it difficult to compete.

Maasai in Tanzania have had similar problems. In the 1970s the government tried to settle the Maasai and destroy their freedom to move from place to place with their herds of cattle. More recently Maasai have been forced to live in smaller and smaller areas. As the population of Tanzania increases, the pressure on the Maasai to settle down is very high.

Tourists in a *manyatta* in the Maasai Mara, Kenya. *Manyatta* are specially built villages where tourists can buy Maasai goods, such as bracelets and carvings. This provides a good source of income, but some Maasai feel it is wrong to exploit their traditions.

65

The Nuer

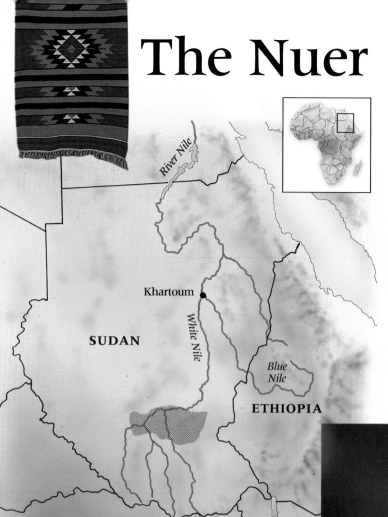

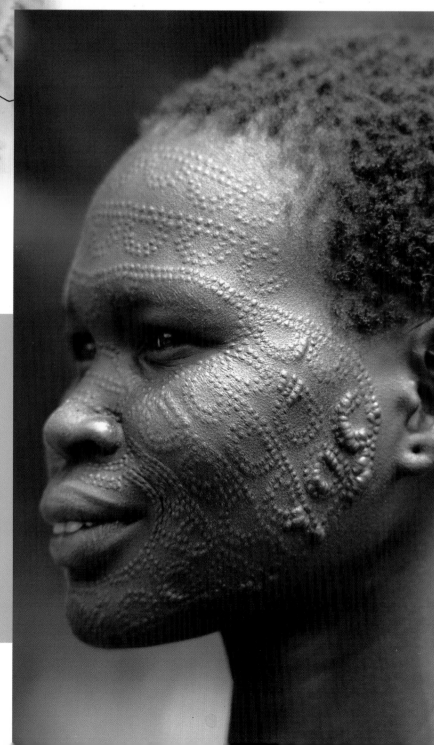

The Nuer live in the southern part of Sudan, which is the largest country in Africa. When Sudan became independent in 1956 the Nuer population was about 300,000. However, no census has been carried out recently and their exact population today is unknown.

Nuer value their equality and their freedom to move from place to place. They used to spend the wet season on high ground, where they could grow crops, and the dry season along the rivers, so they could live by fishing and find water for their cattle. They had no chiefs

Right A Nuer girl with the traditional facial markings of her tribe.

NUER RELIGION

Nuer believe in one god, called Kwoth. The word *kwoth* also refers to the spirits that Nuer say live around them. Some spirits live in the sky with Kwoth, while others live on earth and are symbolized by wild animals. Nuer clansmen make offerings of cattle to Kwoth and to the spirits believed to live on earth. Today many Nuer are Christian, but they mix Christian and traditional beliefs.

but were organized into clans, as well as age groupings similar to those of the Maasai. They frequently stole cattle from their neighbours, and their neighbours would do the same to them.

There has been civil war in Sudan since 1983. Over a million people have been killed, and even more have been forced to leave their homes. In 1989 a military dictatorship took over and swept away the elected government. The Islamic fundamentalists, who now run the Sudanese government, have forced Nuer children to go to school to learn the Koran, the holy book of the Islamic faith. But the Nuer had their own religion, and many wanted to practise Christianity instead of Islam.

In 1991 the army, which opposed the government, split into two sides which began to fight each other. One of these armies, the Southern Sudan Independence Army, includes many Nuer. The other, the Sudan Peoples Liberation Army (Mainstream) is mainly made up of Dinka, the traditional rivals of the Nuer. In one incident in 1993, Dinka soldiers lined up 32 Nuer women and shot them. There have been similar incidents in which Nuer have done the killing. Traditional cattle raiding has given way to warfare with automatic weapons.

A young Nuer boy stands in the ruins of his home, destroyed during factional fighting in the village.

THREATENED BY WAR

Other cultures threatened by war include the Dinka, Koma and Shilluk (Sudan), Somali (Somalia and Ethiopia), Hutu, Tutsi and Twa (Rwanda and Burundi), Kissi (Sierra Leone and Liberia), Saharawi (Western Sahara) and Lunda, Mbundu and Barotse (Angola).

Nuer people living by a tributary of the River Nile at Nasir, southern Sudan.

The Kel Ahaggar

The Kel Ahaggar are a branch of the Tuareg peoples of North Africa. Their home is a dry, mountainous area of southern Algeria and northern Niger. They are divided into two classes: commoners and aristocrats. The Tuareg as a whole number nearly a million, but there are fewer than 20,000 Kel Ahaggar.

All the Tuareg, and their close relatives the Berbers and the Arabic-speaking Bedouin, are at the mercy of the harsh North African environment. They depend on oasis water for their camels and other livestock. Tuareg peoples of Mali and Niger have cattle, but the Kel Ahaggar keep mainly sheep and goats.

The nomadic lifestyle of the Kel Ahaggar is well suited to the desert, but they have experienced serious problems in recent times. Drought in the Sahara has caused the death of many of their animals. In addition, other Tuareg from Mali and Niger have moved into Kel Ahaggar areas because of drought and fighting in their own countries. In the 1980s Kel Ahaggar from Niger tried to settle in Algeria, but

Kel Ahaggar tribesmen dressed up for a festival in Djanet, Algeria.

the Algerian government sent them away. In 1989 Niger agreed to take them back and help them, but they still have not received the aid they were promised.

A Tuareg in traditional dress on his camel. His headdress would give him some protection in the desert against a sandstorm.

The Kel Ahaggar

0   100 200 300 400 500   miles

0   200   400   600   800   km

SPAIN

MOROCCO

ATLAS MOUNTAINS

ALGERIA

Algiers

SAHARA DESERT

HOGGAR MOUNTAINS
Tamanrasset

MALI

NIGER

MAURITANIA

TRADE AND WAR

The Kel Ahaggar are traditionally a warlike trading people. Their weapons include daggers, swords and iron spears, and they carry leather shields. They use these to protect themselves from raiders when they travel. In the past, the Kel Ahaggar attacked other travellers and took their goods in order to use or sell them.

The Kel Ahaggar still try to trade cloth, animal skins and household goods across the desert. Nowadays though, trade is difficult because their camels are no match for modern trucks. Also, governments have tried to stop nomads trading across their national boundaries.

THREATENED BY LOSS OF PASTURE LAND

Other pastoral cultures threatened by drought and loss of their pasture land include the Kel Azjer (Libya and Algeria), Kel Ataram (Mali), Fulani (Mali, Niger and Nigeria), Herero (Botswana and Namibia) and Himba (Namibia).

A camp at the foot of the Hoggar Mountains in Algeria. This will be a temporary stop before moving on again.

ASIA
Central and South Asia

The Asia of Marco Polo, with its caravans running from China to Europe, was a land of numerous different peoples who moved around the great Chinese, Mongol and Persian empires. Central Asia is generally dry, often desert. It is difficult to grow crops, and in the past people kept herds of animals, which they drove from place to place in yearly nomadic cycles to make the best use of the thin vegetation.

A child on a yak led by her mother near Samye, Tibet.

Today many of these peoples live in politically sensitive areas near modern international borders, where they find themselves under pressure to conform to the language and customs of their rulers. Nomadism is disliked by governments because they see it as primitive and because it makes people harder to control. Modern governments often force nomadic peoples to give up their wanderings and live in towns, where it is impossible to keep up their former culture.

For most of this century, much of Central Asia has been under Communist rule. Communist governments taught that there were no gods or spirits, and often persecuted those who practised traditional customs and religions. Although the situation is less harsh than it was, this persecution is still a problem in China.

India and its neighbouring countries in South Asia have high populations and, because of the monsoon rains, a lot of forest. In India alone there are over 50 million people officially classified as tribal, many living by hunting and shifting cultivation in remote mountainous jungles. Here the main threat to indigenous cultures comes from the hunger for land and timber among the large populations of the plains. Forests are cut down for building materials or to make space for rice fields. Firewood is now so scarce that it often costs more than the food that is cooked on it. Conflicts between settlers among the majority Bengali population and indigenous groups have led recently to massacres of indigenous peoples in Bangladesh.

In Myanmar (Burma) violence is destroying the culture of a number of minority peoples. When the British Empire broke up, the non-Burmese peoples of Myanmar were not given the independence they had been promised. Their protests have led to a long-running war being waged against them by the Burmese government.

POISONED

'The government seems to think that no one lives out here in the desert. They test their bombs in preparation for some enemy outside the country. But it's our people who end up getting poisoned by radiation, not them. What's the use of winning wars if your own people are made sick in the process? Is it that it doesn't matter because we're not Chinese?'

A Uigur, in the interior of China

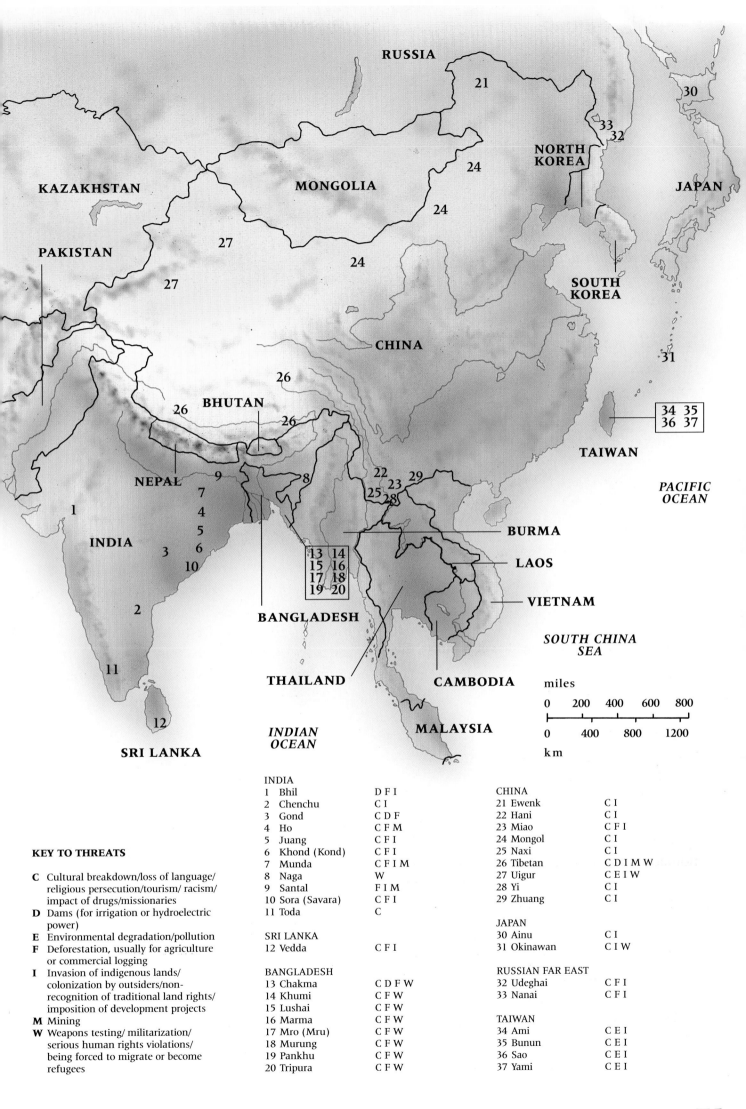

RUSSIA

21

KAZAKHSTAN

MONGOLIA

24

24

PAKISTAN

27

27

27

24

24

CHINA

26

BHUTAN

26

26

NEPAL

9

8

22

23

29

25

28

INDIA

7

4

5

6

10

1

3

2

11

12

SRI LANKA

INDIAN
OCEAN

13 14
15 16
17 18
19 20

BANGLADESH

THAILAND

NORTH
KOREA

33
32

SOUTH
KOREA

JAPAN

30

31

34 35
36 37

TAIWAN

PACIFIC
OCEAN

BURMA

LAOS

VIETNAM

SOUTH CHINA
SEA

CAMBODIA

MALAYSIA

miles

0   200   400   600   800

0   400   800   1200

km

KEY TO THREATS

C Cultural breakdown/loss of language/
religious persecution/tourism/ racism/
impact of drugs/missionaries
D Dams (for irrigation or hydroelectric
power)
E Environmental degradation/pollution
F Deforestation, usually for agriculture
or commercial logging
I Invasion of indigenous lands/
colonization by outsiders/non-
recognition of traditional land rights/
imposition of development projects
M Mining
W Weapons testing/ militarization/
serious human rights violations/
being forced to migrate or become
refugees

INDIA
1   Bhil   D F I
2   Chenchu   C I
3   Gond   C D F
4   Ho   C F M
5   Juang   C F I
6   Khond (Kond)   C F I
7   Munda   C F I M
8   Naga   W
9   Santal   F I M
10 Sora (Savara)   C F I
11 Toda   C

SRI LANKA
12 Vedda   C F I

BANGLADESH
13 Chakma   C D F W
14 Khumi   C F W
15 Lushai   C F W
16 Marma   C F W
17 Mro (Mru)   C F W
18 Murung   C F W
19 Pankhu   C F W
20 Tripura   C F W

CHINA
21 Ewenk   C I
22 Hani   C I
23 Miao   C F I
24 Mongol   C I
25 Naxi   C I
26 Tibetan   C D I M W
27 Uigur   C E I W
28 Yi   C I
29 Zhuang   C I

JAPAN
30 Ainu   C I
31 Okinawan   C I W

RUSSIAN FAR EAST
32 Udeghai   C F I
33 Nanai   C F I

TAIWAN
34 Ami   C E I
35 Bunun   C E I
36 Sao   C E I
37 Yami   C E I

71

Southeast Asia

For thousands of years, the humid forests of Southeast Asia have been home to more indigenous peoples than any other part of the world. These peoples have lived closely with the forest on which they depend. Their religion and social life are intimately adapted to their forest environment, and their cultures respect the rain forest processes of life and growth.

But for thousands of years, Asian civilizations and the farmers who feed their cities have been clearing this rain forest. During the second half of the twentieth century, this process reached a point where it threatens the very existence of the forests and of the peoples who live in them. In many countries, the police and army help farmers to attack the forest peoples and drive them out. The indigenous peoples' traditional use of this land is usually not recognized in law and so they have no rights of ownership.

A further modern threat comes from the massive demand for timber from industry in Japan, Korea and the West. Companies strip the land bare, and deforestation then decreases rainfall, leading to drought and starvation. Meanwhile, mining pollutes the rivers with mercury, lead and other heavy metals. Numerous species of plants are disappearing. As forest peoples are forced to abandon their cultures, thousands of years of accumulated knowledge of what these plants are and how to use them is also being lost.

In many parts of Asia, religious intolerance is also a threat. The region's majority populations belong to the world religions of Hinduism, Islam, Buddhism and sometimes Christianity. These generally regard tribal beliefs, gods and spirits as primitive and try to convert minority peoples or make them feel ashamed of their own heritage.

A major threat to indigenous cultures is schooling. Children are taught the language, beliefs and values of the dominant culture. Many young people then lose the use of their own language, and never return to their own culture. In some countries, cultural conformity is sometimes enforced by military regimes using campaigns of rape, torture, deportation and mass murder. In Irian Jaya (the western half of the island of New Guinea which is now part of Indonesia), resistance to such programmes has dragged local populations from their stone-age cultures

A Papua New Guinean warrior adorned with war paint, shells, feathers and teeth.

FORCED TO MOVE

'Here in Indonesia, they're deliberately exporting people from the crowded central islands of Java and Bali. They're sending them to the thinly populated outer islands. It's disastrous for the small forest tribes there, who lose their forest and their freedom. But it is also miserable for the new arrivals. They're stuck in the middle of nowhere, with no help, in a place where rice can't even be made to grow!'

An anonymous Indonesian critic

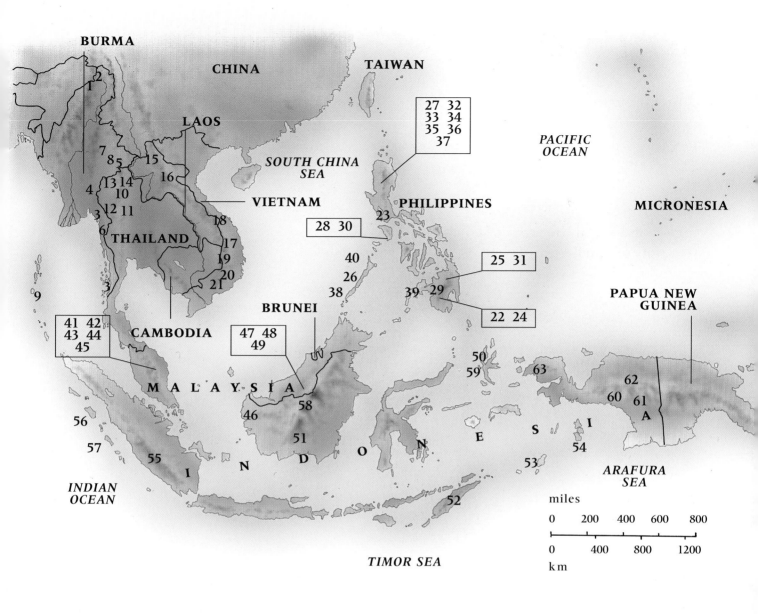

KEY TO THREATS

C Cultural breakdown/loss of language/religious persecution/tourism/racism/impact of drugs and missionaries

D Dams (for irrigation or hydroelectric power)

E Environmental degradation/pollution

F Deforestation, usually for agriculture or commercial logging

I Invasion of indigenous lands/colonization by outsiders/non-recognition of traditional land rights/imposition of development projects

M Mining

W Weapons testing/militarization/serious human rights violations/being forced to migrate or become refugees

MYANMAR (BURMA)

1	Chin	I W
2	Kachin	I W
3	Karen	I W
4	Kayah	I W
5	Lahu	I W
6	Mon	I W
7	Palaung	I W
8	Shan	I W

ANDAMAN ISLANDS (Part of India)

9	Onge	C F I

THAILAND

10	Akha	C F I
11	Hmong	C F I
12	Karen	C F I
13	Lahu	C F I
14	Lisu	C F I

LAOS

15	Lahu	F I W
16	Meo (Miao)	F I W

VIETNAM

17	Bahnar	C F I
18	Bru	C F I
19	Jarai	C F I
20	Mnong	C F I
21	Stieng	C F I

PHILIPPINES

22	Ata	F I
23	Ayta	F I
24	Bagobo	F I
25	Banwaon	F M
26	Batak	F I
27	Bontoc	D F I M
28	Buhid	F I M W
29	Bukidnon	D F I
30	Hanunoo Ibaloy	D F I M W
31	Higaonon	F I M
32	Ifugao	D F I M
33	Igorot	D F I
34	Ilongot	D F I
35	Isneg	D F I
36	Kalinga	D F I M
37	Kankanai	D F I
38	Palawan	F I
39	Subanen	F I
40	Tagbanwa	F I

MALAYSIA

Malay Peninsula (Orang Asli peoples)

41	Batek	C F I
42	Chewong	C F I
43	Jahai	C F I
44	Semai	C F I
45	Temiar	C F I

North Borneo (Sarawak and Brunei)

46	Dayak	F I
47	Iban	D F I
48	Kayan	F I
49	Kenyah	F I

INDONESIA

50	Behuku	F W
51	Dayak	F I
52	East Timorese	C F I W
53	Evav	I
54	Jarjui	F I
55	Kubu	F I
56	Niha	C
57	Sakalagan	C
58	Punan	F I
59	Tobelo Dalam	F I
60	Amungme	C E I M W
61	Dani	C I W
62	Hupla	C I W
63	Moi	C F I W

Tibetans

Lamas playing horns during a Cham ceremony at Ta Gong Monastery in Tibet.

The country of Tibet sits high up in the Himalaya Mountains. Tibetan culture is based on the herding of yaks and other animals, with small areas of millet and other crops grown in the valleys. For centuries, Tibet has been closely linked to the Chinese empire but has had a distinctive culture of its own. The heart of this culture is Buddhism combined with the worship of local spirits. The priests of this religion are Buddhist monks called lamas.

In the 1950s, China invaded and occupied Tibet against strong opposition from the Tibetans. In their campaign against all religions, the Communist government of China persecuted Buddhist monks and nuns, and demolished numerous monasteries. Some lamas accompanied their leader, the Dalai Lama, into exile but those who remain still form a focus of resistance. The government continues its campaign of torture, imprisonment and killing of those who support the lamas.

Today, Chinese soldiers police the towns and Chinese settlers are being moved in to settle the country. The Tibetans are increasingly becoming outsiders in their own homeland. Of all the many minorities in China, the Tibetans are the most intensely persecuted, but because of the worldwide popularity of Tibetan Buddhism, Tibetan culture has many sympathizers abroad. Many Tibetan refugees live in India and in the West, where they try to retain their culture and teach Buddhism to interested foreigners.

ALSO UNDER THREAT

Other cultures in China threatened by religious or ethnic discrimination include the Uigur (Muslim) and Mongol (Buddhist and shamanist).

This holy route in Lhasa, Tibet, was dug up by the Chinese authorities to prevent Tibetans from using it.

0   100   200   300   400   miles

0   200   400   600   k m

CHINA

TIBET AUTONOMOUS REGION

Nanda Devi (7817 m)

HIMALAYAS

Dhaulagiri (8221 m)

Shigatse

Lhasa

Salween River

Tsangpo River

Chengdu

Lithang

Everest (8848 m)

NEPAL

Kanchenjunga (85987 m)

River Ganges

INDIA

BHUTAN

BURMA

BANGLADESH

THE DALAI LAMA

The Dalai Lama is respected worldwide for his preaching of non-violence. He has been awarded the Nobel Peace Prize. The Dalai Lama is said to be a reincarnation of the Buddha himself. Each time he dies, he enters the body of a new child and the lamas (monks) search Tibet for a young boy who shows signs of being this child. After being forced into exile by the Chinese invasion, the present – fourteenth – Dalai Lama has said that he may be the last one. But some people believe that he may now be reborn in another country.

This young Tibetan boy, who has become a monk, has a silver locket with a picture of the Dalai Lama.

Ainu

The Ainu people are now concentrated mainly on the island of Hokkaido in northern Japan, where they work in farming, fishing and the tourist industry. Estimates of their numbers vary between 24,000 and 80,000, since many Ainu are still embarrassed to reveal their identity.

The Ainu language is unwritten, so their history is not recorded. The Ainu emerged as a culture in the early fourteenth century in Hokkaido. Since then, the Japanese have come to dominate Ainu territory. In the nineteenth century, the Ainu lost many of their remaining traditional hunting and fishing rights, took Japanese names and went to Japanese schools.

The Japanese regard the Ainu – with their long beards and distinctive costumes and customs – as primitive and exotic. The Ainu have given up many of these distinctive features, but they sometimes dress up and perform for Japanese tourists. Today, only the very old can remember the songs, legends and rituals of their ancient culture, and perhaps the language will die with them. Marriages between Ainu and Japanese mean that children may become absorbed into Japanese culture.

However, younger Ainu are taking a new interest in Ainu history and a new pride in their ancestry. They are demanding the use of the Ainu language in school textbooks, respect for traditional salmon-fishing rights and an end to racial discrimination.

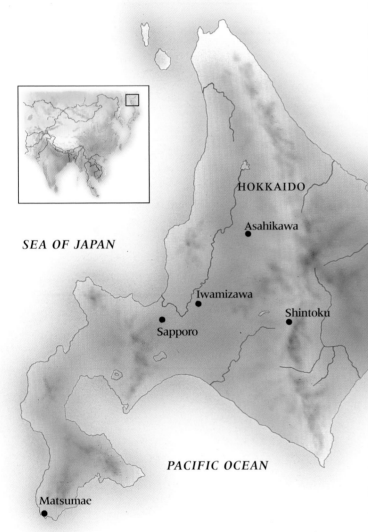

SEA OF JAPAN

HOKKAIDO

Abashiri
Asahikawa
Bihoro
Teshikaga
Iwamizawa
Shintoku
Sapporo
Kushiro

PACIFIC OCEAN

Matsumae

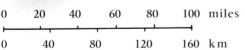

| 0 | 20 | 40 | 60 | 80 | 100 | miles |
| 0 | 40 | 80 | 120 | 160 | k m |

Map, above: Ainu people live throughout the northern Japanese island of Hokkaido.

Ainu elders at the Ashiri Chep Nomi ceremony, held to welcome the first salmon. The ceremony is held in September and is now a statement of the Ainu's separate identity.

A tourist shop in the village of Nibutani, southern Hokkaido. Nibutani is one of the major Ainu villages, considered to be the Ainu cultural capital. A leading elder, Kayano Shigeru, has successfully revived an interest in Ainu culture; he has also become the first Ainu Member of Parliament in Japan.

ALSO UNDER THREAT

Other cultures threatened by assimilation into a large modern society include the Okinawan (Japan) and the Kaoshan peoples – Ami, Bunun, Sao and Yami (Taiwan).

THE AINU BEAR FESTIVAL

The Ainu traditionally raised and sacrificed a bear in the autumn and offered its soul food and saké (an alcoholic drink made from rice), believing that the bear would carry their messages to the spirits. Today, bear ceremonies are still performed, but the bear is not killed. Many Ainu feel that this ceremony is sacred and should not be performed to entertain outsiders, so very few non-Ainu have ever witnessed it.

Mr Kaizawa, the owner of the tourist shop in the picture above, is carving an owl. He uses power tools to get a rough shape before finishing the rest by hand. The owl is sacred to the Ainu.

Buhid

The 7,000 islands of the Philippines have experienced 400 years of Spanish Catholicism and 50 recent years of US influence. These islands contain many small communities of indigenous peoples. The Buhid and their neighbours on the island of Mindoro live scattered in thick jungle. They are unusually peaceful and have no recorded history of warfare among themselves.

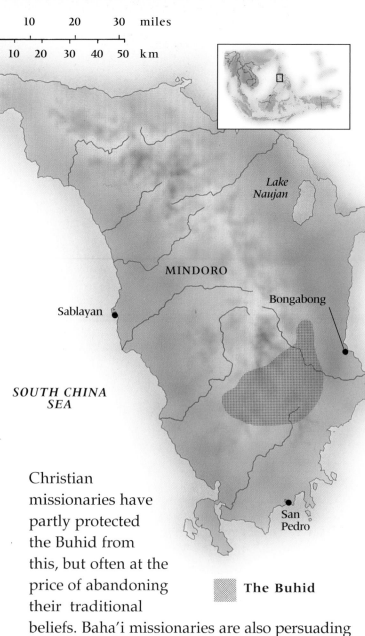

Since the 1960s, logging companies have opened roads into Buhid territory, allowing the land-hungry Christian majority to flood in from the lowlands. The Buhid are often driven off their land or used as cheap labour, while outsiders shoot game, destroy fruit trees and even murder Buhid who protest. Similar problems with loggers and settlers affect indigenous peoples throughout much of Southeast Asia. At first, the Buhid starved or fled to remoter sites. Now, in an attempt to protect themselves and block further settlement by outsiders, they are abandoning their scattered forest way of living and are building bigger villages.

The introduction of money and education encourages young people to be drawn into lowland culture, but it has also given them the necessary knowledge to fight against logging and coal-mining projects on their territory.

Christian missionaries have partly protected the Buhid from this, but often at the price of abandoning their traditional beliefs. Baha'i missionaries are also persuading people to abandon their beliefs.

The Buhid

Since the 1980s, the jungles of Mindoro have become a battleground between Communist guerillas and Philippine government forces.

A group of Communist guerillas passing through Boswak village, in the centre of the Buhid territory. The village is in the upper Fay Valley, where there is a great deal of fighting between the guerillas and government troops.

KNOWING AND USING PLANTS

Forest peoples of the Philippines have a detailed knowledge of plants and how to use them. They can often name more plants than a scientific botanist can, and spend much of their time discussing the shape, colour and smell of different plants and where they grow. As they are forced out of the forest, this knowledge is lost forever.

A mother and child gather seedlings from taro plants for replanting. The taro has large, edible roots.

THREATENED BY DEFORESTATION

Other Southeast Asian cultures threatened by deforestation include the Akha, Hmong and Karen (Thailand), the Batek, Chewong, Jahai, Semai, Temiar, Dayak, Iban, Kayan, and Kenyah (Malaysia), the Behuku, Dayak, East Timorese, Jarjui, Kubu, Punan and Tobelo Dalam (Indonesia), the Bahnar, Bru, Jarai, Mnong and Stieng (Vietnam) and the Bontoc, Hanunoo Ibaloy, Ifugao, Kalinga, Palawan and Tagbanwa (Philippines).

Buhid leaders signing a petition to the government, demanding recognition of their ancestral lands.

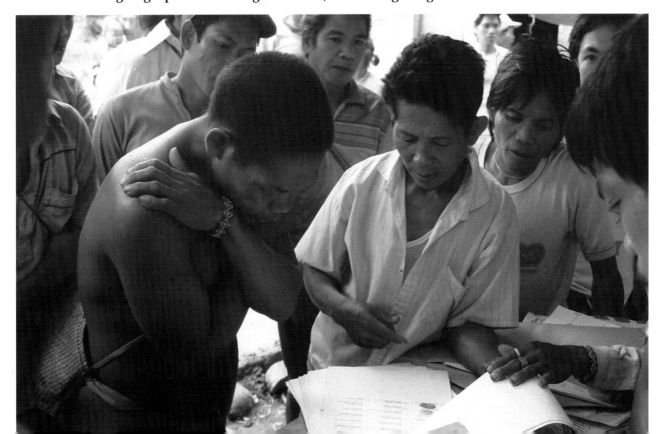

Sora

The Sora number around 400,000 and are one of many tribes in India who live amidst larger Hindu populations. Their culture is based on shifting cultivation in the forest and on a traditional forest religion.

The Sora believe that illness is caused by the spirits of nature and by their own ancestors, and call a female shaman, or spirit medium, to heal them. The shaman goes into a trance and the spirits speak through her and discuss the cause of the illness with the patient. In order to effect a cure, the patient then sacrifices an animal to the spirits.

With pressure from outsiders, the forest has largely disappeared in the last 20 years. The Sora have struggled for a long time to protect their land, but the main threat to their culture now comes from a change in their own attitude.

Sora landscape in the dry season. Trees are felled to create rice fields in the valleys, but soil erosion is causing problems.

ALSO THREATENED

Other cultures in India threatened by culture change or loss of land include the Bhil, Chenchu, Gond, Ho, Juang, Khond, Munda and Santal.

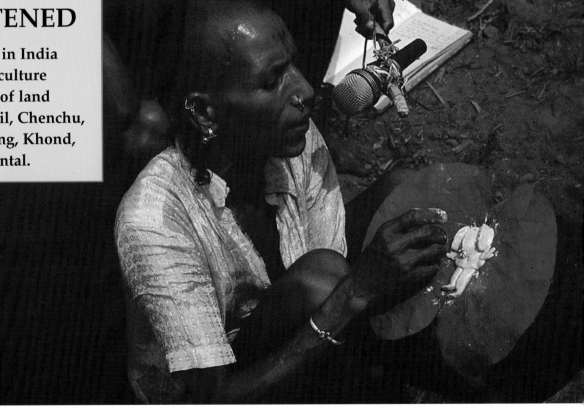

At a funeral, a male shaman makes a model of the deceased woman out of rice flour. This will help the dead woman to give her name back to a new baby in her family.

Young Sora go to school and have started to despise the culture of their parents. Education has taught them to fight for their place in the outside world, so the young Sora are developing a new culture which is more suited to their needs today. Instead of thinking about forest spirits, they now think about passing exams and getting government jobs. Along with this, they are giving up their old religion and becoming Baptists.

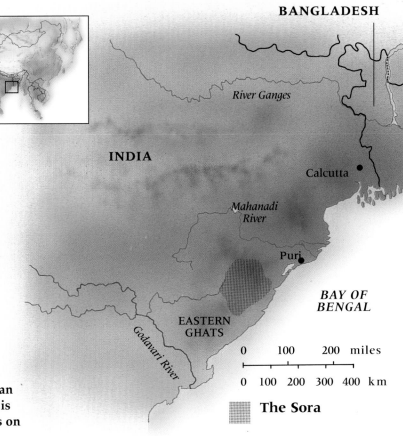

The old lady in the centre of the picture is a shaman in a trance. The spirit of a little boy who has died is speaking through her mouth to his mother, who is on the left hugging the shaman.

SAVING TREES

'Saving the trees is only the first step... Our real goal is to save ourselves. Our future is tied up with them.'

A spokesman for the Chipko movement (a movement among tribal peoples in the Indian Himalayas, whose women began hugging trees to prevent them being cut down by loggers).

THE HEALING TRANCE

A shaman sits on the ground in a state of trance. In front of her sits a young mother holding a sick child. One after another, the spirits of the child's dead ancestors speak through the shaman's mouth. Each spirit denies responsibility for the child's illness. Finally, one ancestor spirit announces that he has made the child ill because the child's parents did not make him enough offerings of rice and wine. 'Everything you eat and drink,' says the spirit, 'you inherited from me. So why do you begrudge me a meal now?' The parents promise to sacrifice a buffalo to the ancestor, and go off to prepare a feast which the whole community will attend.

Amungme

Much of the mountainous interior of the island of New Guinea was not brought under colonial administration until the middle of this century. Now the eastern half of the island is independent and is called **Papua New Guinea**, while the western half, **Irian Jaya**, is ruled by Indonesia.

One group in the west who are seriously threatened are the Amungme, who number 13,000 and inhabit the high Sudirman Mountains. Beneath year-round glaciers, the Amungme live by growing edible tubers and hunting wild pigs and cassowaries.

A US mining company has established massive copper and gold mines on Amungme land. These mines bring profit to the Indonesian government but are a disaster for the Amungme, who have lost their right to hunt, grow crops and even to walk to their own sacred mountain. Amungme complain that they are not able to get education or work and are not allowed to use the shops. Mineral wastes pollute their rivers and many people suffer from copper poisoning. Some Amungme have been forcibly resettled in the swampy lowlands, where they have no livelihood and suffer from the heat. A protest rally was met with a massacre, codenamed 'Operation Annihilation' by the Indonesian army, in which thousands are believed to have died.

As well as being a rich source of minerals, the island of New Guinea also has the most forest

BURN EVERYTHING

The pace of cultural change in New Guinea has been bewildering. Educated young people suffer from culture shock when they return to the villages and have to do hard gardening work and respect their elders. 'The government and the missionaries came and told us to burn everything in the fire,' said one young man. 'They burned the good and the bad things together. Bark-cloth belts and grass skirts are good customs, but they burned these along with sorcery, which was bad.'

A warrior preparing for a Sing Sing ceremony.

82

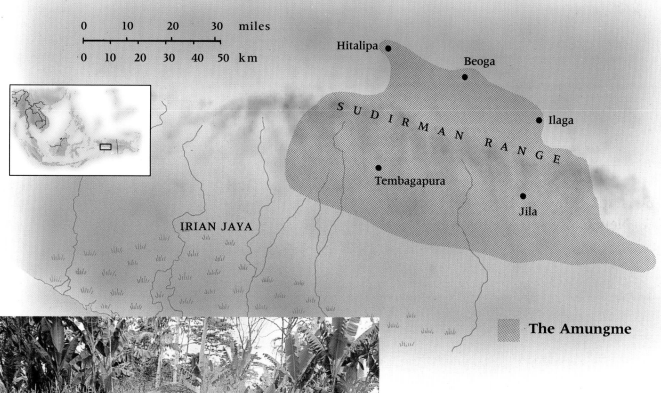

The Amungme

Below Deforestation is a big problem in New Guinea. Here Klinki pines are being felled to provide timber for export.

A pig kill feast. On such ceremonial occasions, pigs are killed and the person holding the feast gives the meat to other members of the group.

per head in tropical Asia and many peoples are threatened by logging. Irian Jaya is also used as a destination for resettled populations from central Indonesia (see page 72). In the independent eastern part of the island, indigenous peoples form the government themselves. Here, many peoples are also threatened by mining and forestry projects, but generally without the same kind of military repression.

ALSO THREATENED

Other mountain peoples in western New Guinea threatened by resettlement in the plains include the Dani and Hupla.

83

AUSTRALIA AND NEW ZEALAND

Australia and New Zealand were unknown to Europeans until just over 200 years ago. But they were home to cultures that had been developing for thousands of years: the Aborigines of Australia and the Maori of New Zealand. Each of these peoples had adapted, down the centuries, to the environment in which they lived and developed complicated systems of beliefs and values.

When European settlers arrived, the balance of life was upset. The Europeans brought with them new ideas about buying and selling goods, the ownership of land, warfare, religion and, perhaps most importantly, new diseases to which the indigenous people had no resistance. Hundreds of thousands died as disease, warfare and competition for the best land began to have terrible effects.

In the 200 years since the arrival of Europeans, some of the problems that faced the Maori and Aborigines have gone away. They are no longer hunted and killed. Their burial sites are not robbed for skulls and skeletons to send away to museums in Europe or America. They are no longer denied the right to vote, and they have a say in the way their countries are run.

> '*We hope to establish a future for Australia, and that future is very simple and clear – White Australia together with Aboriginal Australians, and then we are all Australians.*'
>
> Galarrwuy Yunipingu, Chairman of the Northern Land Council

Many of the difficulties of 200 years ago still exist, though. The most important concern for both Maori and Aborigines is land. Europeans occupied huge areas of land that the native people had been using for thousands of years. In most cases, the indigenous groups are still struggling to get this land back. Even the lands that they have kept are sometimes under threat, from pollution, mining, development, road building and farming.

Today, few Maori or Aborigines still live on the land their ancestors once occupied. Their families were forced to leave years ago, and many now live in towns and cities. Here they have often ended up living in bad housing, with few facilities and little money. In some cases, compensation for land that was taken generations ago could help these communities start schools, cultural associations and other facilities that would keep their culture alive.

Aborigine children sometimes tame wild animals in the bush by feeding them. Kangaroos are quite easy to tame and will allow the children to pick them up.

A Maori carver at work on an ornate wooden carving. Wood carving is an important traditional activity among the Maori of New Zealand. Their work is often highly detailed and it can also be very large.

Australian Aborigines

Aborigines demonstrating at the 200th anniversary of the founding of Australia in Sydney, Australia, in 1986. They are holding a giant Aborigine flag, in which red represents both the ground and Aboriginal blood spilt in over 200 years of white occupation; the gold disc is the sun; and the black symbolizes the Aborigines themselves.

Before Europeans arrived in Australia, there may have been as many as 1.5 million Aborigines spread across the continent. Many lived by hunting and gathering food, others perhaps by farming. The Aborigines had their own complicated religions and social structures, and a deep spiritual link to the land they occupied.

Aboriginal culture was largely dependent on land: land on which to hunt and to gather and grow food. The land is also linked strongly to Aboriginal religion: Aborigines believe that the land was made by ancestral beings, and that these are still a part of the landscape. A hill, a pond (or *billabong*), a rock formation – each could be home to an ancestral being.

Today, Aboriginal groups are battling to regain land taken by non-Aborigines. Large areas of this land is currently owned by the

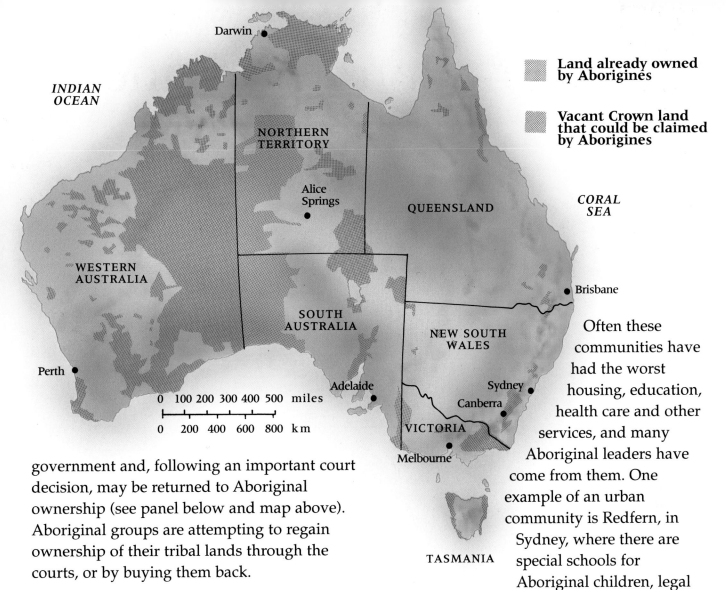

Land already owned by Aborigines

Vacant Crown land that could be claimed by Aborigines

INDIAN OCEAN

Darwin

NORTHERN TERRITORY

Alice Springs

QUEENSLAND

CORAL SEA

WESTERN AUSTRALIA

SOUTH AUSTRALIA

NEW SOUTH WALES

Brisbane

Perth

0 100 200 300 400 500 miles

0 200 400 600 800 km

Adelaide

Sydney

Canberra

VICTORIA

Melbourne

TASMANIA

government and, following an important court decision, may be returned to Aboriginal ownership (see panel below and map above). Aboriginal groups are attempting to regain ownership of their tribal lands through the courts, or by buying them back.

About 15 per cent of Aborigines live in Sydney or Melbourne, Australia's two largest cities.

Often these communities have had the worst housing, education, health care and other services, and many Aboriginal leaders have come from them. One example of an urban community is Redfern, in Sydney, where there are special schools for Aboriginal children, legal and medical services, Aboriginal radio stations and many other facilities.

THE MABO DECISION

In 1992, Australia's High Court decided that Mer (or Murray) Island, in Torres Strait, was owned by the native islanders, not by the Queensland government. The case got its name from Eddie Mabo, one of the tribal elders.

The Mabo Decision is important because, previously, Australian law had been based on the idea that before Europeans arrived in Australia the land was *terra nullius*, or belonged to no one. Now, the court has acknowledged that the land belonged to the tribes that occupied it.

An Aborigine has deliberately set fire to the bush to smoke the animals out. When the creatures leave the safety of the undergrowth he can shoot them.

The Maori

This map shows the traditional lands of the main Maori tribes. Many tribe members no longer live in their traditional tribal areas: instead, they have moved to the cities and towns and live alongside the *pakeha* (their name for non-Maoris). Life is hard for Maori all over New Zealand because of the lack of special educational facilities for their children, the difficulties they have getting well-paid jobs, and the near-impossibility of living a traditional life in a modern, Western country.

1 Muapoko
2 Ngaiterangi
3 Ngapuhi
4 Ngarauru
5 Ngai Mamoe
6 Ngai Tahu
7 Ngati Apa
8 Ngati Awa
9 Ngati Hau
10 Ngati Haua
11 Ngati Kahungunu
12 Ngati Koata
13 Ngati Kuia
14 Ngati Maniapoto
15 Ngati Maru
16 Ngati Paoa
17 Ngati Porou
18 Ngati Rangitane
19 Ngati Rarua
20 Ngati Raukawa
21 Ngati Ruanui
22 Ngati Tama
23 Ngati Toa
24 Ngati Tuwharetoa
25 Ngati Whatua
26 Poutini Ngai Tahu
27 Rangitane
28 Rongowhakaata
29 Taranaki
30 Te Arawa
31 Te Ati Awa
32 Te Aupori
33 Te Rarawa
34 Tuhoe
35 Uriohau
36 Waikato
37 Waitaha
38 Whakatohea
39 Whanau-a-Apanui

The Maori name for New Zealand is *Aoteoroa* – which means the Land of the Long White Cloud. Traditional Maori culture is based on the land; they were farmers who also snared birds, fished and collected seafood. The men fought wars with other tribes, and Maori lived in fortified villages, called *pa*, at the tops of hills.

In 1840, Maori chiefs signed a treaty that said they would give sovereignty over Aoteoroa to Britain, so long as the Maoris kept their rights to farm, hunt and fish. This Treaty of Waitangi was not honoured, and many Maori have lost their tribal lands. Many Maori now live in the cities and try to fit in as well as they can with non-Maoris. In the last few years, the New Zealand government has begun to look again at the way the Maori have been treated. It set up the Waitangi Tribunal to judge the claims of tribes that felt they had been dealt with unfairly. Soon there were 150 cases waiting for the tribunal's attention. The Waitangi Tribunal's first case was that of Aila Taylor, a member of the Te Ati Awa tribe from Taranaki. He was attempting to stop the construction of a petroleum plant, which would have polluted the Taranaki reefs. Aila said that the reefs belonged to his people and that they should be protected under the Treaty of Waitangi. The commission agreed.

The government has had to listen to the Maori and now plans to let the tribes decide how government money allocated to them should be used. Most people in New Zealand realize that the Maori are an important part of their country, and that they cannot be ignored any more.

This spectacular gateway was made by Maori carvers.

A Maori warrior strikes a war-like pose as part of a ritual dance called the *haka*. Displays such as this are usually performed when tribal groups meet.

Further Information

ORGANIZATIONS TO CONTACT

Survival International is a worldwide organization based in London. It publishes an annual review and a newsletter. There is also a Young Survival section, which has produced a *Junior Action Pack*.

> Survival International
> 310 Edgware Road
> London W2 1DY
> Tel: 01207 2421441

Website: www.survival.org.uk

Cultural Survival (CS) is a non-profit organization which publishes a quarterly magazine as well as occasional papers and special reports.

> Cultural Survival, Inc.
> 11 Divinity Avenue
> Cambridge, MA 02138
> USA

The **Minority Rights Group** (MRG) publishes reports on its research findings and works for the human rights of minorities of all kinds, throughout the world.

> The Minority Rights Group
> 379 Brixton Road
> London SW9 7DE
> Tel: 01207 9789498

Website: www.minorityrights.org

BOOKS TO READ

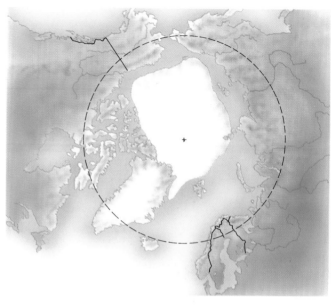

THE FROZEN NORTH

For younger readers

Inuit by Bryan and Cherry Alexander (Wayland, 1995)

The Saami of Lapland by Hugh Beach (Minority Rights, 1988)

The Gaia Atlas of First Peoples by Julian Burger (Gaia Books, 1990)

For older readers

Polar Peoples: Self-Determination and Development Minority Rights Group, eds. (Minority Rights, 1994)

Native Peoples of the Russian Far North by Nikolai Vakhtin (Minority Rights Group report, 1992)

The Inuit (Eskimo) of Canada by Ian Creery (Minority Rights, 1993)

NORTH AMERICA

For younger readers

Canada's Indians and *The Original Americans: US Indians* both by James Wilson (Minority Rights Group reports)

Native Americans (Discoveries series, Macdonald Young Books, 1995)

Native Americans by James Wilson (Threatened Cultures series, Wayland, 1992)

Stories from Native North America by Linda Raczek (Wayland 1999)

MEXICO, CENTRAL AMERICA AND SOUTH AMERICA

For younger readers

The Amazon by Julia Waterlow (Wayland, 1992)

The Amazon Rainforest and Its People by Marion Morrison (Wayland, 1993)

Rainforest Amerindians by Anna Lewington (Wayland, 1992)

We Have Always Lived Here: The Maya of Guatemala by Margaret Burr (Minority Rights, 1991)

For older readers

Indians of the Americas (Survival International, 1992)

The Maya of Guatemala by Philip Wearne (Minority Rights Group report, 1994)

The Mexican Americans by Stan Steiner (Minority Rights, 1979)

AFRICA

For younger readers

The Atlas of Endangered Places by Steve Pollock (Belitha Press, 1993)

Conflict in Somalia and Ethiopia by Patrick Gilkes (Wayland, 1994)

Conflict in Southern Africa by Chris Smith (Wayland, 1992)

Kalahari Bushmen by Alan Barnard (Wayland, 1993)

EUROPE AND THE MIDDLE EAST

There are almost no current books for children on the threatened cultures of this area. Among the few are *Kurds* by John King (Wayland, 1993) and *Bedouin* by John King (Wayland, 1993). *Gypsies* by Thomas Acton and David Gallant is to be published by Wayland in 1996.

The following are adult books from which some useful information might be gained, although many are old and will be hard to find:

Romanichal Gypsies by Thomas Acton & David Gallant (Wayland, 1997)

Roma: Europe's Gypsies by Grattan Puxon (Minority Rights, 1987)

Upon the Doorposts of Thy House: Jewish Life in East and Central Europe Yesterday and Today by Ruth Ellen Gruber (Wiley, 1994)

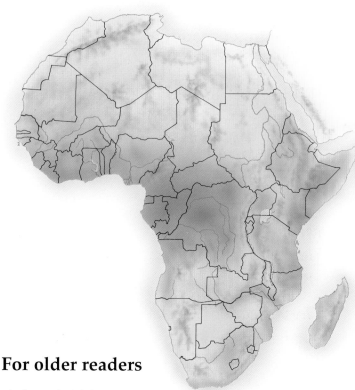

For older readers

Atlas of African Affairs by Ieuan LL Griffiths (Methuen, 1987)

The Falashas: Jews of Ethiopia by David Kessler & Tudor Parfitt (MR, '85)

Populations in Danger by Médicins sans Frontières, edited by François Jean (John Libbey, 1992)

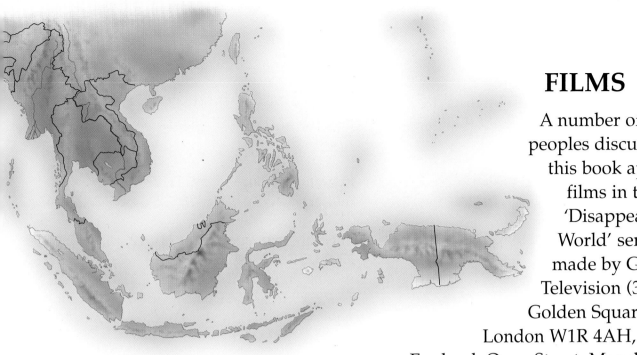

ASIA

For younger readers

There are few books on the threatened cultures of this region. Among the few are: *The Adivasis of India* (Minority Rights, 1999)

For older readers

Minorities of Central Vietnam by Jacques Dournes (Minority Rights Group report 18, 1980)

The Shaman by Piers Vitebsky (Macmillan, London, 1995) [about shamanic cultures worldwide]

AUSTRALIA & NEW ZEALAND

For younger readers

The Maori of Aotearoa/New Zealand by Robert Macdonald (Minority Rights, 1990)

FILMS

A number of the peoples discussed in this book appear in films in the 'Disappearing World' series, made by Granada Television (36 Golden Square, London W1R 4AH, England; Quay Street, Manchester M60 9EA, England; or 400 Madison Avenue, Suite 1511, New York, NY 10017, USA).

Recommended films from the many in this series include the following:

Across the Tracks: Gypsies in Hungary (Hungary, 1988)

The Herders of Mongu-Taiga (Russia, 1989)

The Kayapo: Out of the Forest (Brazil, 1989)j92

Maasai Women (Kenya, 1974)

Maasai Manhood (Kenya, 1975)

The Mursi (Ethiopia, 1985)

The Tuareg (Algeria, 1972)

The Quechua (Peru, 1974)

Index - lifestyles & threats

LIFESTYLES

farmers/agriculturalists 18, 30, 31, 32, 34, 36, 40, 42, 43, 44, 50, 51, 58, 66, 74, 80, 82, 88

hunter-gatherers 8, 10, 11, 14, 16, 19, 20, 22, 24, 26, 28, 40, 41, 44, 45, 60, 61, 62, 76, 86

nomads 8, **8**, 12, 13, 18, 22, 46, 52, 53, 54, 55, 64, 65, 68, 69, 70

urban dwellers 16, 18, 38, 56, 57, 84, 87, 88

THREATS

alcoholism 10, 11, 20, 22
animal rights movements 10, 11, 14
assimilation to majority culture 20, 47, 49, 58, 59, 77

colonists 24, 32, 37, 38, 39, 45, 58, 71
communism, after affects of 11
cultural breakdown 13, 33, 35, 37, 38, 71, 73, 80

dam-building 17, 19, 33, 35, 37, 38, 39, 71, 73
deforestation 62, 71, 72, 73, 80, 81, 83
discrimination 56, 74, 76
disease 9, 18, 20, 24, 28, 32, 36, 38, 40, 58, 59, 84
drought 59, 61, 69

emigrate, pressure to 47, 49
environment, pollution of *see* pollution
environmentalists 10, 11, 14, 15

family breakdown 22
forestry 9, 20, 22, 59, 62, 63, 83

human rights abuses 33, 35, 37, 39, 71, 73
hydroelectric stations 9, 11, 20, 22, 33, 35, 37, 39, 71, 73

land invasion 33, 35, 36, 37, 38, 39, 44, 45, 71
land rights 19, 26, 73

lands, loss of 23, 26, 27, 32, 33, 42, 59, 64, 69, 72, 73, 80, 84
language, loss of 10, 11, 47, 48, 49, 51, 70
logging 11, 19, 24, 33, 35, 37, 38, 39, 62, 70, 71, 73, 78, 83

migrate, pressure to 59, 71, 73
military activity 9, 19, 20, 22, 33, 35, 37, 39, 42, 71, 73
minerals, extraction of 10, 11, 12, 13, 19, 20, 22, 23, 33, 35, 37, 38, 39
mining 9, 19, 20, 29, 30, 33, 35, 37, 39, 40, 41, 71, 72, 73, 78, 82, 83, 84
missionaries 11, 14, 24, 33, 35, 37, 39, 40, 41, 71, 73, 78, 82, 83, 84

nomads, sedentarization of 47, 49

pollution 10, 11, 12, 20, 24, 38, 40, 71, 73, 82, 84, 88
poverty 20

radioactive fallout 10, 11, 13, 17, 70
ranching 35, 36, 37, 38, 45
religions, threat to 14, 19, 20, 47, 49
resettlement 83

sacred sites, destruction of 20, 28
suicide 10, 11, 20, 22, 28

tourism 17, 20, 29, 33, 35, 37, 39, 71, 77

unemployment 20, 28

wars 58, 59, 67, 84
water rights 19, 24, 30

Index - peoples

Peoples who appear in a special feature are indexed in **BOLD CAPITALS**. Photographs are indexed in **bold** numerals.